THE
IMMORTAL
MIND

"In this important and well-written book overwhelming evidence is provided for the continuity of consciousness after physical death. After reading this wonderful book it seems obvious that we are and always will be instantaneously interconnected with each other, because our eternal consciousness will never end; it is beyond time and space. We are then forced to reconsider the never proven hypothesis that the brain produces mind. Highly recommended."

PIM VAN LOMMEL, M.D., CARDIOLOGIST AND
AUTHOR OF *CONSCIOUSNESS BEYOND LIFE*

"Hands down, this is the best collection of evidence from near-death experiences, apparitions, after-death and medium-transmitted communication, past-life recollections, and reincarnation ever put together. Laszlo and Peake skillfully weave all of this into the deeper dimensions of consciousness and creation, what many call the Akasha, to establish the immortality of the soul and the purposefulness of the human experience. Real, irrefutable evidence."

P. M. H. ATWATER, L.H.D., AUTHOR OF
THE BIG BOOK OF NEAR-DEATH EXPERIENCES,
NEAR-DEATH EXPERIENCES: THE REST OF THE STORY,
DYING TO KNOW YOU: PROOF OF GOD IN THE NEAR-DEATH
EXPERIENCE, AND CHILDREN OF THE FIFTH WORLD

"Finally, leading scientific theory meets highly suggestive research for the continuity of consciousness after physical death. As a result, *The Immortal Mind* routs the dead-end dogma of scientific materialism like no other book you'll read."

JAMES O'DEA, FORMER PRESIDENT OF
THE INSTITUTE OF NOETIC SCIENCES (IONS)
AND CEO OF THE SEVA FOUNDATION

"Combined with a discussion of quantum physics, Laszlo and Peake present a convincing case for nonlocal consciousness. A most enthralling read that highlights we are undergoing a very exciting paradigm shift."

PENNY SARTORI, PH.D., RGN, AUTHOR OF
THE WISDOM OF NEAR-DEATH EXPERIENCES

"We are entering in to a new paradigm of understanding consciousness and its relationship with the brain and beyond. In *The Immortal Mind*, Laszlo and Peake provide a concise and lucid overview of the data for consciousness beyond the brain. Exploring a revolutionary new mechanism of consciousness-brain interactions using the principles of modern science such as quantum physics and string theory, this book is a welcome addition to the current paradigm shift of consciousness and a great asset for any student of the subject."

MANJIR SAMANTA-LAUGHTON, M.D., AUTHOR OF
PUNK SCIENCE AND *THE GENIUS GROOVE*

THE
IMMORTAL MIND

Science and the Continuity of Consciousness beyond the Brain

ERVIN LASZLO

WITH ANTHONY PEAKE

Inner Traditions

Rochester, Vermont • Toronto, Canada

Inner Traditions
One Park Street
Rochester, Vermont 05767
www.InnerTraditions.com

Text stock is SFI certified

Library of Congress Cataloging-in-Publication Data
Laszlo, Ervin, 1932–
   The immortal mind / Ervin Laszlo, with Anthony Peake.
      pages cm
   Includes bibliographical references and index.
   ISBN 978-1-62055-303-9 (pbk.) — ISBN 978-1-62055-304-6 (e-book)
   1. Philosophy of mind. 2. Consciousness. I. Peake, Anthony. II. Title.
   BD418.3.L37 2014
   129—dc23
                                                                                    2014013830

Printed and bound in the United States by Lake Book Manufacturing, Inc.
The text stock is SFI certified. The Sustainable Forestry Initiative® program
promotes sustainable forest management.

10 9 8 7 6 5 4 3 2 1

Text design by Priscilla Baker and layout by Debbie Glogover
This book was typeset in Garamond Premier Pro with Trajan Pro and Helvetica
Neue LT Std used as display fonts

To send correspondence to the author of this book, mail a first-class letter to the
author c/o Inner Traditions • Bear & Company, One Park Street, Rochester, VT
05767, and we will forward the communication, or contact the author directly at
ervin@ervinlaszlo.it.

CONTENTS

Part 3

THE EXPLANATION

THE BIG QUESTION

Does our consciousness—mind, soul, or spirit—end with the death of our body?* Or does it continue in some way, perhaps in another realm or dimension of the universe? This is the "big question" thoughtful people have asked throughout the ages.

Let us come down to the bottom line right away. Are we entirely mortal? Or *is there an element or facet of our existence that survives the death of our body?* This question is of the utmost importance for our life and our future.

In one form or another, the idea that consciousness persists beyond the living brain and body has been affirmed in thinking about the nature of reality for thousands of years. It was based, however, on personal insight, handed down on the strength of its intrinsic meaningfulness and spiritual authority. In recent years more solid evidence regarding the "big question" has come to light. Some of it has been subjected to controlled observation, and some of the observations have been recorded. In the chapters that follow we review some of the truly credible and robust strands of the evidence.

---

*We shall use *consciousness* and *mind* interchangeably, while reserving *soul* and *spirit* to the spiritual and/or religious context.

There are three fundamental questions we need to address, and we address each of them in turn.

First, is there such a thing as consciousness not associated with a living brain? There appears to be "something" that can be experienced on occasion, and even engaged in communication, and it appears to be the consciousness of a person who is no longer alive. We review the robust strands of the evidence in this regard in part 1.

Second, assuming that there is "something" we can experience that appears to be a discarnate consciousness, what does this mean for our understanding of the world—and of the human being in the world? Who and what are we, if our consciousness can survive our body? And what kind of a world is that in which consciousness can exist beyond the brain and the body? These are the questions we take up in part 2.

Third, what kind of explanation do we get for the possible persistence of consciousness beyond the brain and the body, and for contact and communication with such a consciousness, when we confront the evidence with the latest insights coming from the natural sciences? This is the question we ask in part 3.

These tasks are ambitious, but not beyond the scope of science. We know that conscious experience can occur in the temporary absence of brain function: this is the case in so-called NDEs—near-death experiences. Could conscious experience occur also in the *permanent* absence of brain function—when the individual has died? It makes sense to ask this question as well, because it is important, meaningful, and not without observational evidence.

Mainstream science—the science taught in most schools and colleges—does not confront these questions: it denies the very possibility that consciousness could exist in the absence of the living organism. However, unlike the Ten Commandments Moses brought to his people, the tenets of mainstream science are not engraved in stone. In its next development science could expand its scope to investigate phenomena that address these questions. And when it does, it is likely to reach insights that are of vital interest not just to scientists, but to all people in the living, and perhaps not entirely mortal, human community.

PART 1

THE EVIDENCE

*Consciousness
beyond the Brain*

1
NEAR-DEATH EXPERIENCES

Could human consciousness exist in the absence of a living brain? There is credible evidence regarding this question, provided by persons who had conscious experience while their brain was clinically dead. They reached the portals of death but came back. Their conscious experience is known as NDE: the near-death experience.

NDEs tell us that conscious experience is possible during the time the brain is temporarily dysfunctional. Temporary cerebral dysfunctions may occur in cases of severe illness or brain damage, where signs of cerebral activity cease but are subsequently recovered. If the time without brain functions does not exceed a critical threshold—counted in seconds—the brain can regain normal functioning. Then the consciousness that was previously associated with that brain can reappear.

Conscious experience during the time the brain is clinically dead is an anomaly. It is not accounted for by the current materialist paradigm in science, where conscious experience is considered a product of cerebral functions. That paradigm maintains that when those functions cease, the consciousness they have produced ceases as well.

However, evidence furnished by documented cases of NDEs show that consciousness does not always cease when the brain is clinically dead. Conscious experience during this critical period is not always recalled, but recall occurs with significant frequency; in some studies in 25 percent of the documented cases. Moreover, the recall is often veridical: it embraces things and events a person with normal brain functions would have experienced at the given time and place.

In the last forty years there has been a growing fascination with the NDE. Numerous survivors of cardiac arrests, car crashes, and severe illnesses have reported conscious experiences. There was no widely recognized name for this experience, nor was any modern book written on it, until Raymond Moody published his *Life After Life* in 1975 and suggested "near-death experience" as the generic name for it. Moody amassed a large collection of firsthand reports by people who returned from a near-death state, and he was struck by the consistency of the reports. He noted that the experience includes several core features, and these he termed "traits." The basic traits are: a sense of being dead; peace and painlessness; the out-of-body experience*; the tunnel experience; encounters with family members and other people from one's environment; rapid rise into the heavens; a reluctance to return; the past-life review; and encounter with a being of light.

Reports of such experiences can be found throughout history. One of the oldest reports of a near-death experience is described by Plato in the Tenth Book of the *Republic* written around 420 BCE. Plato describes the experience of Er, a Pamphylian soldier who was killed in battle. His body was returned to his home village for cremation. It was noted by his family that even after ten days the body was showing no signs of decay. However, two days later they proceeded with the ceremony. As the body was placed upon the funeral pyre Er suddenly

---

*In an out-of-body experience a person has veridical perceptions from a position outside and above his or her body.

revived. He excitedly informed the mourners that he had "seen the world beyond." Plato wrote:

> He said that when his soul went forth from his body he journeyed with a great company and that they came to a mysterious region where there were two openings side by side in the earth, and above and over against them in the heaven two others, and the judges were sitting between these, and that after every judgement they bade the righteous journey to the right and upward through the heaven with tokens attached to them in front of the judgement passed upon them, and the unjust to take the road to the left and downward, they too wearing behind signs of all that had befallen them, and that when he himself drew near they told him that he must be the messenger to mankind to tell of that other world, and they charged him to give ear and to observe everything in the place.[1]

Plato described how Er journeyed and arrived at a place where he met with disincarnate entities who were judging him. There were, Er said, many others beyond himself ("a great company"). After the judgment, for reasons unknown, Er was informed that he must go back and inform the living of what he had witnessed.

In recent years the NDE has been subjected to controlled observation and scientific assessment. Michael Sabom, a cardiologist specialized in the resuscitation of cardiac arrest victims, examined the cases he treated in regard to the recurrence of the basic NDE traits. He found that of the seventy-eight patients he interviewed thirty-four (43 percent) reported an NDE, and of them 92 percent experienced a sense of being dead, 53 percent the out-of-body experience, 53 percent rising into heaven; 48 percent saw a being of light, and 23 percent had the tunnel experience. All his patients who had an NDE reported a reluctance to return.[2]

Current interest in NDEs has been sparked by a clinical study carried out over more than two decades by Dutch cardiologist Pim van Lommel. Van Lommel conducted standardized interviews within a few days of resuscitation with survivors of cardiac arrest, patients who had recovered sufficiently to recall and recount their experiences. He asked them whether they could remember the period of unconsciousness, and what they recalled of that period. He coded the experiences reported by the patients according to a weighted index. Van Lommel found that 282 out of 344 patients had no recollection of the period of cardiac arrest, but 62 reported some recollection of what happened during the time they were clinically dead, and of these 41 had a "deep" NDE. Half of the patients who had an NDE were aware of being dead and had positive emotions. Among them 30 percent had a tunnel experience, observed a celestial landscape, or met with deceased persons. A quarter of these had an out-of-body experience, communicated with "the light," or saw colors, 13 percent had a life review and 8 percent perceived the presence of a border.[3]

A study by Bruce Greyson in the United States involved 116 survivors of cardiac arrest. Eighteen of the patients reported memories from the period of cardiac arrest; of these, 7 reported a superficial experience and 11 had a deep NDE. Greyson concluded that a clear sensorium and complex perceptual processes during a period of apparent clinical death challenge the concept that consciousness is localized exclusively in the brain.[4] British researchers Sam Parnia and Peter Fenwick concurred. The data suggest, they wrote, that near-death experiences do arise during unconsciousness. This is surprising, because when the brain is so dysfunctional that the patient is deeply comatose, the cerebral structures that underpin subjective experience and memory must be severely impaired. Complex experiences should not arise or be retained in memory.[5]

A SAMPLING OF
DOCUMENTED CASES OF NDE

A wide variety of cases testify to the presence of consciousness during a period when the subject is clinically brain-dead. A remarkable case was reported in August 2013. The British media was woken out of its late summer torpor by a piece of "breaking news." It concerned the unexpected results of experiments carried out on the brains of rats by Dr. Jimo Borjigin of the University of Michigan and a team of researchers. The results of the experiments were published in the *Journal of the Proceedings of the National Academy of Sciences.*

"This study, performed in animals, is the first dealing with what happens to the neurophysiological state of the dying brain," said the study's lead author, Dr. Borjigin. "We reasoned that if near-death experience stems from brain activity, neural correlates of consciousness should be identifiable in humans or animals even after the cessation of cerebral blood flow."[6]

Borjigin's team anesthetized each rat and, by artificial means, stopped its heart. At that point the rat's brain had no blood flow, which means no access to oxygen. For a brain to function, it needs energy, the energy supplied by oxygen carried by the blood. Yet it was clear from the results that not only was there brain activity where none was expected, but there was greater activity than in a normal waking brain. This suggests that before death there is a surge of activity in the brain. The brain appears to be processing information and may be presenting an experience to consciousness.

An early report on human NDE concerns the experience that took place in November 1669, in Newcastle upon Tyne in the North East of England (or, in some reports, in South Wales). The report is in a religious pamphlet written by Dr. Henry Atherton and published in London in 1680. Atherton's fourteen-year-old sister, Anna, had been ill for some time, then was thought to have finally died. The woman attending to her used the only method available at the time for ascertaining death: placing a mirror to her mouth and nose. There was no evidence of breathing. They then placed red hot coals to her feet and received no response. She was clearly in a state of what would now be termed "clinical death." However, she subsequently recovered. When she was able, she described how she had visited heaven and was guided there by an angel. This being showed her:

> "things glorious and unutterable, as Saints and Angels and all in glorious apparell." She heard "unparalel'd Musick Divine Anthems and Hallelujahs." She was not allowed to enter Heaven but the angel told her that "she must go back again for a while, and take leave of her friends, and after short time she should be admitted."

As predicted by her "Angel," Anna died four years later and according to the pamphlet she departed "with great as[s]urance of her happiness hereafter."[7]

While she was in her near-death state, Anna reported seeing people she had known, all of whom had died. There was one individual who, as far as Atherton knew, was alive. However, he subsequently discovered that this individual had passed on a few weeks earlier.[8]

The earliest known systematic research into experiences in which an individual comes close to death yet survives was undertaken by Swiss geologist Albert Heim in the 1870s. As a keen mountaineer, Heim had heard stories from his associates of strange states of consciousness experienced when falling as a result of a climbing accident. His interest was stimulated by his own brush with death in 1871 when he fell seventy feet from a cliff face in the Alps. He said that as soon as he realized what was happening, time began to slow down, and he slipped into an altered state of consciousness. He describes this state as follows:

Mental activity became enormous, rising to a hundredfold velocity. . . . I saw my whole past life take place in many images, as though on a stage at some distance from me . . . Everything was transfigured as though by a heavenly light, without anxiety and without pain . . . Elevated and harmonious thoughts dominated and united individual images, and like magnificent music a divine calm swept through my soul.[9]

This experience was perceived in great detail, although it seems to have taken place in a microsecond of actual time:

I saw myself as a seven-year-old boy going to school, then in the fourth grade classroom with my beloved teacher Weisz. I acted out my life as though I were on a stage upon which I looked down from the highest gallery of the theater.[10]

During a time interval estimated at around three seconds, Heim had experienced a review of his life.

A Celebrated Case and a Celebrity Case

Following the publication of Moody's *Life After Life* in 1975 interest grew in near-death experiences, and many cases were reported. One of the most celebrated cases was that which took place in April 1977 at Seattle's Harborview Medical Center in the state of Washington.[11] A social worker, Kimberly Clark, had been asked to attend to a female migrant worker who was recovering from a massive heart attack. Clark was told that the woman, known as Maria, had suffered two cardiac arrests, the second of which took place in the hospital while she was recovering from the first. Specialist staff had been on hand, and Maria had been successfully resuscitated.

Maria was fully conscious when Clark entered her room. Indeed she seemed to be in a state of excitement. In faltering but precise

English Maria explained that she had experienced a strange series of sensations while she was unconscious. She described how she witnessed her resuscitation from a position outside and above her body, noting printouts flowing from the monitoring machines measuring her vital signs. She then said that something caught her attention outside. From her new location near the ceiling she could see above the canopy of the hospital entrance and in doing so could see something odd. She decided to investigate. By force of will she found herself outside and floating in midair.

As Maria came to terms with what was happening she found that she was able to maneuver herself and look round. She noticed that the mysterious object was located on a third-floor window ledge at the far side of the hospital. Again by force of will she found that she could project herself through space to be next to the object. Much to her surprise she discovered that what had caught her attention was a man's tennis shoe, specifically a dark blue left-foot shoe with a worn-out patch over the little toe and a single shoelace tucked under its heel. With this image in her mind she found herself back in her body as the crash team brought her back to life.

Kimberly was fascinated by Maria's account and agreed to try to see if Maria had actually seen something that existed outside her imagination. She walked outside the hospital but could see nothing from ground level. She then reentered the building and began a room-to-room search of the floor above that where Maria's resuscitation took place. Kimberly could not see anything, even when pressing her head against the window to get a better view. Eventually, and to her great surprise, she did find the shoe. She entered one particular room on the third floor of the north wing and spotted the shoe, although from the vantage point of inside the hospital, she could not see the worn-out toe and the tucked-in shoelace. Clark later managed to retrieve the shoe and was able to confirm that the toe was, indeed, worn out as Maria described. Clearly the proof that the shoelace had been "tucked in" would have been lost as soon as the shoe was moved.

In August 1991 another case was reported; this time, not only were the circumstances surrounding the experience witnessed by medical professionals, but also the extreme physiological conditions that facilitated the experience had been purposively created by them.[12]

Thirty-five-year-old celebrated singer Pam Reynolds had suffered a basilar artery aneurysm. A large artery at the base of her brain had developed a blockage, causing it to fill with blood and expand like a balloon. It was in danger of bursting, which would have resulted in her death. Immediate action had to be taken. However, the location of the aneurysm was extremely problematical.

In order to surgically clear the blockage, the blood supply to the artery first had to be stopped. The surgeons would then be able to open her skull, clear the blockage, and do any necessary repair on the artery and surrounding tissue. This process would need at least one hour to complete successfully. But it is known that any disruption of blood supply to the brain longer than a few minutes will lead to fatal consequences. A recently developed process known as "standby" offered the physicians a solution. Standby involves giving the patient a general anesthetic; when this has taken effect, the patient's body is slowly cooled down, bringing about a form of suspended animation. The heart is then stopped and the blood is drained out of the head; all brain functions come to a halt. The patient is "flatlined"—no measurable electrical activity shows up on the electroencephalogram. The patient is, in effect, brain-dead.

The operation on Pam Reynolds was successfully completed, and Pam survived to live another nineteen years. However, she had an experience while she was in a state of zero brain activity. When her brain returned to normal functioning she described in detail what had taken place in the operating theater, including a description of what music was played (*Hotel California* by The Eagles). She described a series of conversations that took place. She reported having watched the opening of her skull by the surgeon from a position above him, describing in detail the "Midas Rex" bone-cutting device and the distinct sound it made. Yet during that time, in each of Pam's ears there was a specially designed ear-speaker that shut out all external sounds. The speakers were broadcasting audible clicks, used to confirm that there was no activity in her brain stem. She should not have been able to hear anything. Moreover, she had been given a general anesthetic and should have been fully unconscious.

As she heard the bone saw activate, about ninety minutes into the process, Pam saw her body from the outside and felt herself being pulled into a tunnel of light. At the end of the tunnel she saw her deceased grandmother and other deceased relatives. Then she was told by an uncle that she had to return. She felt him push her back into her body, and, on entering it, she described her experience as like "diving into a pool of ice-cold water. . . . It hurt."[13]

The Case of Will Murtha

A relatively recent NDE involved a young man by the name of Will Murtha. In the autumn of 1999 he decided to take a bicycle ride along the seawall near his home in Dawlish on the south coast of England. The tide was extremely high that evening, and the weather was stormy. Waves were crashing into the wall at regular intervals. Suddenly a large wave came over and knocked him off his bike. He pulled himself up off the ground, but as he did so a second wave crashed in and swept him off the wall into the sea.

After a few seconds Will managed to rise up to the surface. He was a strong swimmer and, as a semiprofessional sportsman, also a fit young man. However, as he looked up at the high seawall he knew that getting out of the water would not be easy. He then realized that the tide was going out. He felt himself being drawn out into the deeper waters of the River Exe estuary. Evening was drawing in, and there was nobody to be seen. The lights of Dawlish blinked on, but nobody was looking out to sea. Will knew that he was in trouble. He started to shout for help but to no avail. He began to feel the icy cold of the water gnawing at him. He could keep himself afloat until his energy ran out, but he could not stop the hypothermia. He felt the intense cold make its way up his body. He realized that his body was shutting down; he was dying.

Then he felt an intense feeling of peace come over him. He looked up at a group of seagulls circling above. He realized that he was part of them and they were part of him. He then looked back at the ever-receding seawall and knew that that was part of him as well. He realized that everything was related like one single consciousness. There was a flash of light, and the sea and the cold disappeared.

He found himself running across a road in East London. It was a hot summer's day, and he was paying no attention to anything or anyone. He was back as a child. For a second he felt confusion, and then he heard the squeal of brakes. He looked up to see the front of a car moving toward him at high speed. He had no chance of getting out of the way. He looked above the hood and saw the face of a young woman gazing at him in horror. He heard a sickening thud, and all went black.

Then he was in the hallway of his house in Dawlish. It took him a moment to realize that he was hovering near the ceiling. There was a knock on the door. He watched his wife and daughters walk down the hall and open the front door. Standing there was a police officer. He listened intently as the police officer explained that a body had been washed up on the beach at Dawlish and they had reason to believe that the dead person was a Mr. William Murtha.

The scene faded, and he was back in the water, waiting to die. He had experienced a flashback to his own childhood when he had been hit by a car. He had forgotten the details, but he had reexperi-enced the event in full detail. He had also shared the horror and the guilt of the woman who had hit him. He knew why she had failed to stop in time. She had noticed a ladder in her stocking and was dis-tracted. He realized that he had seen the future, or a possible future, if he failed to get out of the water soon.

Fortunately, Will Murtha was spotted that evening by somebody looking through a telescope. He was pulled out of the water with broken ribs and a severe case of hypothermia. But he survived. The policeman didn't knock on his front door to give the news of his decease.[14]

Nurse Penny Sartori's Reports

In winter 2006 a paper was published in the *Journal of Near-Death Studies,* the peer-reviewed periodical of the International Association of Near-Death Studies. Entitled *A Prospectively Studied Near-Death Experience with Corroborated Out-of-Body Perceptions and Unexplained Healing,* it was a review of the evidence that during cardiac-arrest-stimulated near-death experiences, some subjects report that they have found themselves in an out-of-body state, and during this state they have been able to observe what is going on around them. Usually the vantage point has been near the ceiling of the room or operating theater. The lead author of this paper was Penny Sartori, the young nurse who, on her first night on a ward, had encoun-tered a patient seeing his mother just before he died. With a PhD in near-death studies, Penny was keen to test both the veridical nature of the out-of-body state and the healing aspects of such an experience.

A series of NDEs were reported to Penny by patients surviving a close brush with death. In one case a woman had lost consciousness after an operation. Penny was with her when she came around. The woman described how she had seen her dead mother in a tunnel of light. She was told that it was not her time and she must go back. Another woman, recovering from a life-threatening asthma attack, told the young nurse that during the attack she had been overcome with a great feeling of calmness and peace and then found herself floating above her body lying on the bed. She then floated across the room and toward a cupboard in the corner. As she floated above the top of the cupboard she noticed a mouse trap on the top. The next thing she knew she was floating toward a bright white light. Within the light she could see figures moving. They communicated with her that she needed to go back. This she did and on regaining conscious-ness she informed the nurse about the mousetrap on the top of the cupboard. A porter was called to come with a ladder. On climbing the ladder and viewing the cupboard from above, he was able to confirm that there was, indeed, a mousetrap on it, a mousetrap that was totally out of view for anybody of normal height.[15]

Over a period of five years Penny conducted a prospective study at the Intensive Therapy Unit (ITU) at the Morriston Hospital in Swansea, South Wales. She placed hidden symbols on top of each patient's cardiac monitor attached to the wall beside the bed. This was above head height, so could not be seen by any patient lying in bed or, indeed, standing up. To ensure that the symbols were only viewable from above she concealed them behind ridges on the monitors. One particular case involved a sixty-year-old man who was recovering from complications subsequent to surgery for bowel can-cer. Soon after the operation he had developed blood poisoning and multiorgan failure, but it seemed that he was on the road to recovery. He was sitting in a chair next to his bed when a nurse noticed that he was in some distress. It was at this stage that Penny was called in to assist. In her article she described her actions:

> The senior author (P.S.) then manually ventilated the patient with
> 100 percent oxygen provided by means of an Ambu bag, and
> the drop in oxygen level was rectified. Although his oxygenation
> remained stable above 94 percent, the patient's blood pressure

then dropped to 85/50 millimeters of mercury, his skin became very clammy, and his condition deteriorated rapidly. There was a brief episode of supraventricular tachycardia that reverted spontaneously without any medication. . . . By the time he was put into bed he was deeply unconscious, his eyes were closed, and he was not responding to verbal command or deep painful stimuli.[16]

This was of great concern to the physiotherapist who had been responsible for persuading the patient to get out of bed and sit in the chair. Penny wrote that the therapist stood outside the bedside screens, nervously and intermittently poking her head around to check on the patient.[17] When the patient's condition had been stabilized, it was noticed that he had been drooling. This was cleaned by a nurse, first using a long suction catheter and then a pink oral sponge soaked in water. For thirty minutes the patient showed no signs of alertness and it took three hours for him to fully regain consciousness.

However, when he did, he was in a state of excitement. He was unable to speak as he was still attached to the ventilator and was given a letter board by the physiotherapist. What he spelled out stunned all present, including a group of doctors and nurses. "I died and I watched it all from above." Unfortunately Penny had been called away, but when the patient had recovered, Penny interviewed him. He reported,

All I can remember is looking up in the air and I was floating in a bright pink room. I couldn't see anything; I was just going up and there was no pain at all. I looked up the second time and I could see my father and my mother-in-law standing alongside a gentleman with long, black hair, which needed to be combed. I saw my father—definitely—and I saw this chap. I don't know who he was, maybe Jesus, but this chap had long, black, scruffy hair that needed combing. The only thing nice about him was his eyes were drawing you to him; the eyes were piercing; it was his eyes. When I went to look at my father, it was drawing with his eyes as well, as if I could see them both [at] the same time. And I had no pain at all. There was talking between me and my father; not words but communicating other ways—don't ask me what, but we were actually talking. I was talking to my father . . . not through words through my mouth, but through my mind . . . [18]

I could see everybody panicking around me. The blonde lady therapist boss, she was panicking; she looked nervous because she was the one who got me out in the chair. She hid behind the curtains, but kept poking her head around to check on me. I could also see Penny, who was a nurse. She was drawing something out of my mouth, which looked to me like a long, pink lollipop, like a long, pink thing on a stick—I didn't even know what that was.[19]

The patient was then told that he had to go back, as he was "not ready yet."

Amanda Cable's Return

A still more recent report contains many of Moody's traits with one curious feature. It appeared in the English newspaper *Daily Mail* in November, 2012, written by the journalist Amanda Cable. She described how, on Wednesday, September 4, 2003, she was rushed to the hospital with an unexpected ectopic pregnancy (that is, a baby was growing in one of her fallopian tubes). By the time she arrived at the hospital it was discovered that she had suffered an internal hemorrhage. She was given morphine and placed in an upstairs ward for the night. At 3:30 a.m. the next morning she woke up in agony. A doctor quickly realized that there was something seriously wrong. She drifted in and out of consciousness. Then she reported,

I felt my entire body being sucked up into the white light above. I found myself in a white tunnel—and I knew I had died. Away from the cursing of the medics and the bleeps of the machines, there was a wonderful sense of calm. Instead of awful pain, I felt light and clear-headed. I knew what was happening but I felt no fear. I knew I had to join my loved ones who were already on the other side. It was a tranquil and warm acceptance. But I also became aware of somebody standing a few feet away from me. I turned, expecting to see my grandmother, who had passed away some years earlier.[20]

However, Amanda then perceived that standing next to her was not her grandmother, but her daughter Ruby. That very day five-year-old Ruby was to start her first day at school. The previous evening Amanda had been distressed that her health crisis would mean that she would miss her daughter's big day. She had tearfully sent her husband, Ray, home from the hospital with strict instructions not—under any circumstances—to ruin Ruby's great day, and that he should make sure that her uniform and hair were in perfect order. But here was Ruby in the role of a "being of light." She was standing next to her mother in her new school uniform with her hair tied neatly in bunches. Amanda reported,

I was pleased but mildly surprised. I'd never seen her in her uniform, and she'd never allowed me to put her hair in bunches. She smiled and took my hand. "Come with me, Mummy," she implored. I followed her down the white tunnel. She kept turning to check that I was behind her. "Quick Mummy," she urged. At the end stood a gate. I stopped, feeling an urge to walk back down the tunnel, where I was sure my beloved grandmother and other family members who'd passed away would be waiting to greet me. But little Ruby was insistent. "Mummy, step

through the gates NOW!" Her urgency bought me to my senses.
I stepped through it and Ruby slammed it shut behind me.[21]

The next thing Amanda knew she was waking up in intensive
care. She was still very ill, but her experience had convinced her
that she would survive, which she did. A few hours later Ray arrived
clutching a photograph of Ruby taken at the school gates. There
she was in her school uniform. It was then that Amanda noticed her
daughter's hair. She had obviously allowed her father, for the first
time, to place her hair in this earlier much-disliked style. The little girl
in the picture was a mirror image of the child that had insisted that
Amanda not cross the threshold into the place of no return.

THE NDE:
WHAT THE EVIDENCE TELLS US

The great variety and frequent occurrence of conscious experience
during periods when the brain has been clinically dead suggest that
consciousness can persist in the temporary absence of brain function.

Objections of many kinds have been raised to this proposition,
and some appear well taken. It turns out, for example, that the "tunnel
experience" and the appearance of a bright light at its end may be due
to a sudden rush of blood to the brain. As among others, Borjigin's
already cited experiments have shown this is known to occur when
the organism is entering a critical phase near death. However, veridical perception in many cases of NDE has no standard explanation.
This perception occurs in the absence of measurable brain activity, yet
it matches (or even exceeds) the clarity of the perception the subject
would have had in a normal state of waking consciousness.

NDEs do not occur in all cases when individuals who were at the
threshold of death return to life. But this is not a serious objection.
First, because NDEs do occur in a significant number of cases: for

example, as we have seen, van Lommel reported that 62 out of 282 patients in his Dutch Prospective Study reported an NDE. Second, because a report on a near-death experience is a recall of an individual's past experience and such recall does not happen in every case. Even vivid experiences can be forgotten, or recalled only in altered states of consciousness.

The significant fact about the NDE is that conscious experience takes place during the time when the brain is clinically dead. This has been sufficiently documented and can be regarded as being beyond reasonable doubt.

2

APPARITIONS AND AFTER-DEATH COMMUNICATION

The NDE tells us that conscious experience can occur during the time the brain is clinically dead. The evidence on this score is robust, for it is in the form of firsthand reports by people who themselves had the experiences. The question we now raise is whether consciousness can persist also when the brain is fully and permanently incapacitated. Can consciousness exist beyond death?

Reports on this score are necessarily less robust than reports of NDEs, since they are not reports of experiences the subjects themselves had, but reports by another person—apparently, the consciousness or "ghost" of a person—who is no longer living. These experiences come partly under the heading of apparitions and visions and partly under that of after-death communications, a term popularized by Bill and Judy Guggenheim in their book *Hello from Heaven*.

Apparitions, visions, and deathbed visitations are widespread. Nonincarnate beings appear suddenly and communicate with the living, sometimes producing information that is later verified. In most cases the apparition is a recently deceased individual, a friend or a member of the family. Raymond Moody collected numerous cases of such "visionary encounters with departed loved ones."

Encounters with the dead have been an element of popular culture for centuries. From Shakespeare's dramatic entrance of Banquo's Ghost in *Macbeth* to the saccharine-sad circumstances of the encounter between lovers in the movie *Ghost,* these encounters have been regularly featured in fiction. However, there are also reports of encounters with the dead in which factual information, unknown at the time to the living witness, has been transferred.

In 1959–60 Dr. Karlis Osis conducted a massive survey in which he asked thousands of health-care professionals across the United States about the deathbed visions of their patients.[1] He received 640 replies based on the observation of 35,000 dying patients. Such was the success of this study that others soon followed. In recent years researcher Emily Williams Kelly has reported that 41 percent of dying patients in her study reported a deathbed vision.[2]

Although the phenomenon has been known for centuries, the first systematic study was undertaken by the Society for Psychical Research in 1882. The results were published two years later in Volume X of the *SPR Proceedings.* This was followed up by similar research in the United States and by the French astronomer Camille Flammarion. In 1925 Flammarion published a hugely influential work titled *Death and Its Mystery,* in which he presented scores of cases of spontaneous contact with deceased individuals.

In May 1988 Bill and Judy Guggenheim created the ADC Project, the first in-depth research into this phenomenon. They collected more than 3,300 personal accounts from people who firmly believed that they had been contacted by loved ones who had died. Their book *Hello from Heaven* describes this project and contains 353 of the most powerful accounts.

In most cases contact is spontaneous, but it can also be intentionally induced. Induced contact and even communication with the deceased is a relatively recent phenomenon. It is not the same as contact and communication through a psychic medium, because the induction of the phenomenon is limited to creating an appropriate state of consciousness in the experiencing subjects themselves. Once this state has been attained, the subjects can communicate on their own. Psychotherapist Allan Botkin, head of the Center for Grief and Traumatic Loss in Libertyville, Illinois, claimed that he and his colleagues had successfully induced after-death communication in nearly three thousand patients.[3]

According to Botkin, ADCs can be induced in 98 percent of the people who try them. The experience usually comes about in a single session. It makes no difference what the experiencers believed prior to their after-death communication, whether they were religious, agnostic, or atheists. It is not limited to a personal relationship with the deceased. Combat veterans can experience contact with an enemy soldier whom they killed but never knew.

There is no need for the psychotherapists to guide their subjects: it is sufficient that they induce the required altered state of consciousness. They then hear their patients describe communication with a deceased person they knew and are grieving for, hear them insist that their reconnection is real, and note that they shift from a state of grief to one of elation and relief.

SOME CASES OF
SPONTANEOUS APPARITIONS
AND AFTER-DEATH COMMUNICATION

In the 1840s interest regarding the ability of the dead to communicate with the living shifted from vague reports of ghosts and apparitions to a seemingly concerted attempt by the dead to open channels of communication with the living.

The new phase began in 1848 with events in a small house in

Hydesville, New York.[4] The Fox family had moved into the house a few years before. It had already gained a local reputation for being haunted. One evening in March of that year the young daughters of the family, Kate and Margaret, claimed that they had been hearing knocking noises and that the knocks or raps would respond to instructions. For example, they had asked the source of the sounds to tell them their respective ages. A series of twelve raps followed by a series of fifteen identical noises were heard. The interest was such that within a few days neighbors were listening in to hear this wonder. Quickly a code of communication was developed by the girls. In this way the entity could give messages. The girls called the spirit "Mr. Splitfoot." Later, through the code, the spirit identified itself as being the ghost of a traveling peddler called Charles B. Rosa, who had had his throat cut in the house five years before by somebody called Charles Bell. The raps then informed the girls that his body had been buried ten feet under the cellar floorboards.

The following summer the cellar was dug up and human remains were found at a depth of five feet. This was an intriguing development, but was it proof of actual spirit contact?[5]

The events at Hydesville spawned a public fascination with ghosts and spirits. This was fanned by the mass media of the day feeding the demand by supplying sensational stories of hauntings and communications with the dead. Authors also quickly spotted an opportunity, and many books were written telling chilling tales of horror and dread. This soon spread across the Atlantic and by the early 1880s a whole entertainment industry had developed to fulfill the public need for sensationalism.

It was against this background of confusion that Sir William Barrett, professor of physics at the Royal College of Science in Dublin, arranged a meeting of scientists, scholars, and spiritualists to discuss this growing social phenomenon. The group met for the first time on February 5, 1882, and after a complex and detailed discussion they agreed to set up an organization to scientifically investigate the claims being made regarding mediumship and the survival of consciousness after the death of the body. They agreed that this new organization would be called the Society for Psychical Research (SPR). One month later, on February 20, 1882, the society was formally constituted under the presidency of Henry Sidgwick, a Cambridge University professor of classics. The council consisted of eighteen members, which included Barrett himself, noted classical scholars F. W. H. (Frederic William Henry) Myers and Edmund Gurney, clergyman and celebrated medium W. Stainton Moses, outspoken skeptic Frank Podmore, and another eminent classical scholar called W. H. Salter.[6]

The group immediately started researching the evidence for survival, and in 1886 a book, written by Gurney, Myers, and Podmore, was published. Titled *Phantasms of the Living,* this huge volume consisted of over 1,300 closely investigated cases of after-death visitations, ghostly manifestations, and other allied phenomenon. Many of the cases involved what were termed "crisis apparitions." For Gurney, Myers, and Podmore this was evidence that something else was involved, and they concluded that this was a form of telepathy.

Subsequently Eleanor Sidgwick, the wife of the SPR president Henry Sidgwick, designed a questionnaire, which was distributed to 17,000 people. This asked whether, during waking life, the respondent had ever heard a disincarnate voice, seen a vision of somebody who had died, or perceived any sensations that seemed to have no physical cause. The results showed that 1,684 people had experienced at least one of these sensations. Of these 300 involved visions of individuals who had died. What was of particular interest to the SPR was that of these 300 cases 80 involved a visitation from a person who had died in the previous twelve hours. Of even more significance was that in 32 of these incidents the person receiving the visitation was unaware of the fact that the associate perceived had died.[7]

Apparitions: Three Cases

Early one morning an unnamed colonel of the Royal Artillery was visited by the ghost of a close friend who had just been killed in South Africa. In the early hours of January 29, 1881, the colonel was awoken from sleep with a start. He looked round his bedroom, and in the dim, early dawn light he saw a figure standing between his bed and a chest of drawers. Straight away he recognized that it was one of his fellow officers, Major Poole. The figure was somewhat disheveled and had a full black beard. It was wearing the standard uniform of the British army when engaged in warmer climates. This included a khaki jacket and a white pith helmet. For a second or two the colonel was confused. He and Poole had been stationed together in Ireland a few years before, and in his semiwakened state the colonel thought he was back in barracks:

> I said: "Hello, Poole! Am I late for parade?" Poole looked at me steadily and replied: "I'm shot." "Shot." I exclaimed. "Good God! How and where." "Through the lungs." replied Poole, and as he spoke his right hand moved slowly up the breast until the fingers rested upon the right lung.[8]

Poole explained that he had been sent forward by his general, and then he pointed toward the window and vanished. Later that morning the agitated and disturbed colonel visited his London club and described to his fellow officers what had taken place earlier. The next day he read in a newspaper that Major Poole had been killed at the Battle of Laing's Neck at exactly the same time that the apparition appeared in his bedroom. Intrigued, the colonel was keen to discover what uniform type Poole was wearing at the time of his death, whether he was bearded (which he had never been in the 23 years in which the two men had been friends), and, finally, the nature of the fatal wound.

Subsequent research by the Society for Psychical Research confirmed that Poole had been shot through the right lung as indicated by the apparition. He had been "sent forward" by his commanding officer, and he was also heavily bearded.

The most intriguing element of the story is the uniform. The British Army had only recently, and somewhat hurriedly, replaced the traditional bright red tunic with a less conspicuous khaki color. Also a brand new innovation, only used until that time in the Transvaal, was the "Sam Browne," a leather belt with a leather strap over the shoulder. In his description of the apparition the colonel stated that Poole was wearing a "brown leather strap . . . crossed his breast. A brown leather girdle, with sword attached on left side and revolver case on the right, passed around his waist."[9]

The second case of an apparition was reported by Eleanor Sidgwick in April 1890 via a Mr. A. B. Wood. Wood had interviewed a woman by the name of Mrs. Agnes Paquet and subsequently checked the facts with her husband, Mr. Peter Paquet.[10]

According to Wood's report Mrs. Paquet had awoken at her normal time of around 6:00 a.m. on the morning of October 24, 1889. For some reason she felt very "gloomy and depressed." Later, after her husband had gone to work and her children had left for school, she decided that maybe a strong tea would raise her spirits. She entered the pantry, and as she did so she saw an image of her brother Edmund in front of her. He was standing with his back to her and seemed to be in the act of falling forward with two ropes, or a loop of rope, wrapped around his legs. Later she described to her husband the image:

> I stated that my brother, as I saw him, was bareheaded, had on a heavy, blue sailor's shirt, no coat, and that he went over the rail or bulwark. I noticed that his pants' legs were rolled up enough to show the white lining inside. I also described the

appearance of the boat at the point where my brother went overboard.

At 10:30 that morning Peter Paquet received a telegram from Chicago delivered to his office. In it he was informed that his brother-in-law, Edmund Dunn, had been drowned in an accident while serving as a fireman on a tug called the *Wolf*. At 3:00 a.m. that morning he had been entangled in a towrope and had been thrown overboard. He immediately made his way home to inform his wife of the bad news. However, he decided to break the news softly and on arrival, announced to her that her brother was sick and in a hospital in Chicago. Agnes replied that she already knew that he was dead and that he had drowned. She then added the precise description quoted above. She then described the appearance of the boat where Edmund had fallen overboard.

Peter Paquet left his wife at home and made his way to Chicago to find out more about the incident. On arrival at the docks he quickly found the *Wolf* and was surprised to discover that his wife had described the part of the vessel in which the accident had taken place with stunning accuracy. As neither he nor Agnes had ever seen the tug before, this was quite amazing to him. He then spoke to the crew, and they confirmed that Agnes had described perfectly what her brother was wearing as he was dragged overboard:

> They said that Mr. Dunn had purchased a pair of pants a few days before the accident occurred, and as they were a trifle long before, wrinkling at the knees, he had worn them rolled up, showing the white lining as seen by my wife.[11]

It was later confirmed by another crew member that Edmund had been caught by the towline in the way described by his sister and had been thrown overboard.

Mrs. Paquet's description of her brother's image was almost holographic in its quality. She was able to perceive precise details about his clothing and, more importantly, also perceived the towrope that brought about his death. There have long been discussions regarding the clothing of ghost images. If it is simply the soul that is returning, how can inanimate clothes also "return from the dead" when they were never alive in the first place? But here we have something more complex in that the towrope also was part of the spectral image. This all suggests that what Anna Paquet saw that morning in her pantry was not a ghostly messenger with intentions to communicate the circumstances of his death to his sister but some form of recorded image that had manifested within the visual field of a young woman.

The third case of an apparition was in Eleanor Sidgwick's 1885 survey. It recounts the case of a woman who was on her deathbed. Having been an extremely organized individual, she was focused on her business interests. However she suddenly stopped and announced that she could hear angels singing. She then seemed puzzled. She stated, "but it is strange, there is one voice amongst them I am sure I know, and cannot remember whose voice it is." At this she pointed away from the bed announcing with surprise, "Why there she is in the corner of the room; it is Julia X."

Julia "X" was a trained singer who had been employed by the woman six or seven years previously to work with some local children. The arrangement lasted a week, and then Julia moved away from the area to get married. It was therefore surprising to all concerned why this woman had appeared in the dying woman's hallucination. The next day, February 13, 1874, the woman died. The following day, on February 14, an announcement was made in the London *Times* that Julia "X" had recently passed away.[12]

The Paquet and the Julia X cases present evidence that a living person can, under certain circumstances, perceive information regarding the death of another. At no time during the spectral encounter between Agnes and Edmund do the actions of Edmund suggest that he is sentient or motivated. There was, however, a case in which information presented by the departed was so strong that it stood up in a court of law.

The Chaffin Case

This case took place in 1925 in North Carolina.[13] On November 16, 1905, James Chaffin of North Carolina drew up a will whereby all his property, an estate of some 102 acres, was to be left to his third son, Marshall. Although witnessed by two friends, the contents of this will were only shared with Marshall and his wife, Suzie. It seems that he changed his mind, and in 1919 he wrote a second will, which he placed inside the family Bible. In this he requested that the property be divided equally between the four sons with the proviso that they look after their mother. He neglected to tell anybody about this second will, nor did he have it witnessed. However, it was in his handwriting, and according to the law of North Carolina, this made it valid. On September 7, 1921, Chaffin, then aged around seventy, died as a result of a fall.

As nobody knew of the second will, all the property went to his surviving third son. Things then took a curious turn. In 1925 Chaffin's second son, James "Pink" Chaffin, began to have a series of dreams in which his father appeared to him. Initially it involved just an image of the father. However, in one dream the image of James Chaffin spoke. The dream figure stated, "You will find my will in my overcoat pocket." Pink checked out where his father's coat had gone and discovered that his mother had given the overcoat to his elder brother, John, who lived twenty or so miles away. In July 1925 Pink and his daughter Estelle, together with a family friend, Thomas Blackwelder, drove over to John Chaffin's house, explained about the dream, and the two of them decided to check the coat. There was nothing in the pockets, but they felt something in the lining. Sewed in was a small handwritten note with the words "Read the 27th Chapter of Genesis in my Daddy's old Bible."

On finding their grandfather's Bible, a prize possession of the deeply religious James Chaffin Senior, in an upstairs room, the brothers checked the pages of the twenty-seventh chapter. The pages had been folded over and inside them was found the 1919 will. Of possible significance was that chapter 27 of Genesis is a parable about how one brother cheats another out of his inheritance.

Marshall had died of heart disease on April 7, 1922, barely a year after his father; his wife, Susie, had inherited everything. Not surprisingly, she contested the second will. A court case ensued, and the 1919 will was produced in court. Chaffin's widow agreed that it was her husband's writing, and the surviving brothers naturally concurred. In a surprise move Susie also accepted that the writing was indeed that of her father-in-law. It seems that a deal was done whereby Susie would have an equal share as the widow of the deceased Marshall. Judgment was given, and the 1919 will stood. Later the second son wrote:

> Many of my friends do not believe it is possible for the living to hold communication with the dead, but I am convinced that my father actually appeared to me . . . and I shall believe it to the day of my death.[14]

A year or so later the Society for Psychical Research instigated an investigation into this seemingly powerful proof of postmortem survival. In 1927, after a thorough investigation, the local lawyer employed by the SPR wrote to them in London stating that the will was genuine and the story, although improbable, was true. However, the honorary officer of the SPR, W. H. Salter, was far from convinced. He believed that the eldest brother, John, with the assistance of the third brother, Abner, had faked the will and fooled Pink into believing he had seen his father's ghost. Salter suggested that John had secreted himself in Pink's bedroom one night wearing his father's overcoat. Since then this case has been written about time and time again. It remains one of the most enigmatic and powerful cases of survival after death ever recorded.

Cases of Deathbed Visions and Visitations

As already noted, Penny Sartori is recognized as one of the leading researchers on near-death experiences. When she was a trainee nurse, Sartori was about to do her first night shift. As the hand-over from the evening shift was taking place, she was informed by one of her associates that one patient was expected to die within two to three hours. Penny was quite surprised by the certitude of the statement and asked her fellow nurse why she believed this to be the case. "Because he is talking to his dead mother" was the reply. Penny checked on the man a few times in the next hour or so, and on each occasion he was staring out with his eyes clearly focused on something in the room that only he could see. He was mumbling under his breath as if holding a conversation with somebody. He seemed happy and positive. As predicted, he died that night.

This introduction to terminal care nursing was so profound that over the years she kept a close watch on the facial expressions and general behavior of patients as they approached the end. Some would be gesturing at somebody that could not be seen, or suddenly a look of recognition would appear on the dying person's face as if they were seeing a long-lost loved one. What Penny observed was nothing new. Such things had been noted for at least a century before her encounter with the unknown. Indeed it was in 1882 that Frances Power Cobbe published a book that discussed the way in which the dying have a glimpse of the next world while they are still in this one.

Cobbe called the book *The Peak in Darien,* a reference to the poem of the same name by John Keats in which the Spanish conquistadors, led by Cortez, look out from a peak in Darien (now Panama). Instead of seeing the expected vista of jungle stretching off to the horizon they see an unknown ocean, the Pacific. For Cobbe, certain glimpses of the next world sometimes involve a strange fact: the dying person reports seeing somebody who, unknown to him or her, had already died.[15]

In 1926 Sir William Barrett of the SPR published a book entitled *Death-Bed Visions.* One case cited in the book was particularly remarkable. It involved a young woman called Doris, who was dying of a hemorrhage after the birth of a child. As she drifted in and out of consciousness, she had a vision of her father approaching her. He had been dead a few years, and clearly she perceived this as a message from beyond that it was her time to die. The concerned medical staff decided that drastic action was needed to bring her out of this morbidity. Her baby was brought to her in an attempt to make her wish to live. This had the desired effect in that it brought about a crisis. Doris felt obliged to stay for the sake of her newborn baby but was also aware that a wonderful new world was available to her.

At this stage the circumstances could be seen as a kind of dream sequence. She knew that her father was dead, so this is not surprising. However, she then saw her sister, Vida, join her father in her vision. This confused Doris because as far as she was concerned Vida was still alive. What she didn't know was that Vida had actually died three weeks earlier but, due to her condition, Doris had not been informed. Barrett was so impressed by the apparition of Vida that he started a systematic study, which was then published in his book.[16]

The Neil Allum Case

In early 2013 an event was described to one of the authors of this book that was a classic case of after-death communication, but it was conveyed through a telephone answering service.[17]

Neil Allum was a long-distance truck driver from Bootle in Liverpool. He had been licensed to drive HGVs (Heavy Goods Vehicles) for more than eighteen years. He enjoyed his job, but it did mean that he was away from his family, partner Lee Mainey and their two sons, for days on end. Normally his journeys from the UK to Europe did not bother him. However, something was on his mind the weekend of the 10/11 of September 2005. He dug out all his insurance papers and discussed in great detail what he wanted to happen at his funeral. This was odd; Neil was only thirty-nine years of age and in good health. Indeed he and Lee had set a date for the following April to get married.

Neil was not alone with regard to this feeling of foreboding. Lee's sister Donna Marie Sinclair had similar sensations. She kept getting images in her mind of a policeman in a luminous jacket knocking at Lee's front door with bad news. Donna could not shake these spontaneous images and discussed them with her cousin. She was a practical, down-to-earth housewife with no interest in anything supernatural. However, for many weeks as she later described it she had sensed a "knowingness" every time she looked at Neil. Many years before Donna and Neil had made a pact in that if he ever got himself in trouble he would discuss it with her on the telephone. Indeed over the years he had called Donna twice to ask her advice and help.

On Monday, September 12, Neil drove off in his truck for a short return trip to the Netherlands. The journey was uneventful until something terrible took place within a few miles of his home. On the outskirts of Liverpool two motorways, the M57 and the M58, join another major road, the A59 at a place called Switch Island. This had been, for many years, a notorious traffic bottleneck. Roadworks had recently started to improve the situation. Of possible significance is that Neil had many times said to his work associates and family members that Switch Island was a deathtrap. As he entered the roadworks in the early hours of Wednesday, September 14, Neil's truck hit the concrete barriers at the side of the road, crushing the driver's cabin. After being cut out of the wreckage, Neil was pronounced dead at the scene.

A police officer in a luminous jacket called at Lee's home in Bootle to give her the news. Lee phoned Donna, and immediately Donna rushed to her sister.

Over the next two weeks Donna was involved with the issues that result from a case of accidental death. She finally returned home on September 28. Waiting for her on her home telephone was a series of messages from concerned friends and relations, plus a confused message from her daughter's midwife (Donna's daughter was pregnant at the time). This was on the digitized answering service BT 1571, hosted on British Telecom computers. After a few rings all calls are diverted to this service. To ensure accuracy of call recording, the service is linked directly to a clock that is always 100 percent correct, since the service is digital and interference is impossible. Donna began to work her way through the calls; each message was date and time stamped. She was informed that the next message was received at 2:15 p.m. on Saturday, September 17, 2005. She was somewhat surprised to hear loud crackling and distortion reminiscent of static. What she heard next was a male voice that said, "It's Neil, is Donna there please?" The message was then broken up by more static and distortion. Then a female voice appeared, "Hello, are you there? I must have a crossed line." Donna immediately recognized both voices. The first was definitely Neil, and the second was the midwife. The message then ended.

Donna immediately contacted the British Telecom fault-line. She was told that crossed lines were impossible with this service and that the dates and time recordings were always accurate and had no relationship with the receiving phone. Thus even if Donna's house had had a loss of electricity this would only reset the clock on the local handset and would have no influence on the BT service. Donna told the technician that accuracy in this case was impossible since the person on the recording had been killed three days before the recording. The technician became quiet for a few seconds and then replied with the comment, "You will be surprised to know that it has happened before," and advised her to do a web search on phone calls from the dead.

Donna was still not convinced. She concluded that it must have been some delay caused by Neil's cell phone; perhaps the message had been held up by the cell-phone-messaging service. She discussed this with the police, only to discover that both of Neil's cell phones had been shattered by the impact of the crash. However, as part of their investigation, the police had done a forensic check of the SIM card and found that the last call Neil had made to Donna's home number had been nineteen days before.

It appears that phenomena of visions and apparitions are not exceptional. Recently deceased persons seem to appear on occasion to the living, and even to communicate with the living.

APPARITIONS AND ADCS: WHAT THE EVIDENCE TELLS US

Contact with deceased persons is a widespread phenomenon; it occurs in most cultures and in various epochs in history. Indigenous people recognized their contact with deceased relatives: their cultures speak of contact with ancestors whom they honor and venerate as if they were living. In the modern world such contact is an anomaly: it has no credible explanation. Affirmations that deceased persons can have consciousness and can be contacted are "esoteric."

For the modern mind apparitions and after-death communication are questionable occurrences, if not outright delusions. They suggest belief in communication with an immortal soul or spirit. A credible explanation of how consciousness could persist beyond the brain would overcome both the skeptical and the religious preconceptions. Many more apparitions, visions, and instances of after-death communication would be experienced by ordinary people and reported without fear of ridicule and without recourse to religious doctrine.

But even given a credible secular explanation, the phenomena may still turn out to occur only in some cases and not in others. It may be that conditions are relatively rare where both the communicating deceased entity and the living receiver are in a state appropriate for communication. "Spiritual" and "transpersonal" phenomena are known to occur primarily in altered states of consciousness, and these states are not common in the modern world.

However, it is not the frequency of after-death contact and communication that concerns us, but their actual occurrence. That such contact and communication can take place is strongly suggested by the evidence. The evidence shows that in some cases "something" that manifests a sense of self and carries memories of physical existence, and on occasion appears clothed in a physical body, is communicating with a living individual. This "something" may be what the spiritual and religious traditions call spirit or soul, and what popular lore regards as ghosts. We can consider it a form of consciousness. We conclude that there is credible evidence that on occasion "something" that appears to be the consciousness of a person who is no longer living manifests itself to a living individual.

3

MEDIUM-TRANSMITTED COMMUNICATION

In chapter 2 we reviewed cases where contact with a deceased individual comes about spontaneously, or else is induced by shifting the living subject into an altered state of consciousness. We now look at cases where such contact occurs through a medium. The medium is usually in the altered state of consciousness known as a "trance" and is channeling the messages and intuitions he or she receives. The process is not essentially different from spontaneous or induced cases of contact, except that a third entity is added. Rather than the subject himself or herself being in an altered state of consciousness, it is the medium who enters such a state. The subject—known as the "sitter"—is in a normal state, listening to the messages or, if they are committed to paper, reading them.

The same question arises in regard to medium-conveyed communication as for direct contact with a no longer living person. What level of credibility can we attach to the evidence that communication with a deceased person actually takes place? Since it is not the subject himself or herself who experiences this communication but a third person, this is a difficult question to decide. Is the third person truly reporting on what he or she is experiencing? And is his or her

41

experience truly originating with the non-incarnate communicator? Is it conceivable that the report originates with a living person and is transmitted to the medium in an undisclosed way, perhaps through extrasensory perception?

To attain adequate credibility we need cases where the evidence excludes these possibilities. This is not to ask for absolute certainty, for in regard to empirical phenomena there is always an element of uncertainty. But if we find at least a handful of cases where the level of credibility approaches reasonable certainty, we will have obtained evidence that something anomalous is experienced by the medium. We shall review here some cases of medium-transmitted communication where this level of certainty, if not absolutely attained, is at least approached.

THE VARIETIES OF MEDIUM-TRANSMITTED COMMUNICATION

Medium-transmitted communication with deceased persons falls into two basic categories: physical transmission and mental transmission. The evidence for physical transmission is through observable events supposedly produced or transmitted by the medium, such as raps, the movement of objects, and the materialization of objects, and occasionally even of discarnate individuals. This type of evidence is problematic because it is highly open to fraud—many if not all such manifestations require complete or nearly complete darkness. It is also problematic because there is no presently conceivable scientific explanation for the physical effect produced by the communicating entity, or by the medium who channels that entity. For these reasons we do not include in this review phenomena such as the materialization of persons or objects and similar physical effects.

Evidence for medium-based contact with deceased persons through mental transmission is more tractable. This kind of evidence comes in various degrees of clarity and complexity. The simplest and clearest form is clairvoyance: the medium, in a relatively normal state of consciousness, claims to see or hear some of the deceased friends or relatives of the sitter and transmits contact with them. Contact may be in plain language or through signs or occurrences that symbolize the meaning of the communication.

A more complex yet at the same time more common form of mental mediumship requires that the medium enter a state of trance. In these instances the medium's consciousness appears to be dominated by a foreign intelligence that takes control over his or her speech, writing, and possibly also behavior. In the most intense forms of this kind of transmission the medium's mind and body seem completely possessed by the foreign intelligence. For example, when Mrs. Leonora Piper, a widely known medium in Boston, entered a trance, she could be cut, pricked, even have a bottle of ammonia held under her nose without producing an effect. Within minutes of entering the trance she would speak with the voice of the foreign intelligence.

Trance mediums seem to have the ability to sense, hear, and see things that are beyond the sensory experience of ordinary people. These abilities are known as clairsentience, clairaudience, and clairvoyance. Some "transfiguration mediums" can even take on the physical form of the communicating entity.

THE RISE OF CONTROLLED
MEDIUM-TRANSMITTED COMMUNICATIONS

The Hydesville events (described in the previous chapter) gave rise to a new social phenomenon—"spiritualism"—which very quickly became something of a religion in America, with large numbers of individuals claiming to be able to speak to the dead and manifest physical evidence of the presence of spirits.

Spiritualism soon spread from America to Britain. The popular media were caught up in the enthusiasm with sensationalistic reports of psychic happenings in séances. By the 1870s genuine mediums were mixing with fraudulent individuals seeking to profit from the new vogue. Newspapers advertised products that could be used by mediums and spiritualists to create illusions to fool the public. Mediumship was becoming a mass spectacle similar to the magic acts performed at the music halls.

It was in the context of this frenzied climate that the Society for Psychical Research was set up by Sidgwick, Barrett, Gurney, Moses, Podmore, and Myers. The initial work of the society was to investigate spontaneous communication between the dead and the living. The 1848 events in Hydesville suggested spontaneous communication with a disincarnate entity. There was no question of lucrative "mediumship" regarding the Fox sisters. It was only later, under the tutelage of Leah, their elder sister, that Kate and Margaret began to manifest what one could recognize as mediumistic skills.

The SPR and its American version, the American Society for Psychical Research (ASPR), which was founded in 1885, became fascinated by mediumship in all its variations and over the years investigated the abilities claimed by many of the most famous mediums.

The first medium to be investigated under controlled conditions was James Eglinton. In the early days many differing forms of communication were used by mediums. One of the most popular was "automatic writing." It was believed that under certain conditions a spirit or disincarnate entity could take control of the medium's hand and write messages, letters, and even whole books. Usually a pencil and paper were used, but in the case of Eglinton it was a piece of chalk and a slate. It was clear that the two researchers, a young Australian, Dr. Richard Hodgson, and Eleanor Sidgwick, the author of the questionnaire discussed in the previous chapter, were far from convinced; they said so in an article published in the *Journal of the Society for Psychical Research*, the academic journal of the ASPR. This caused a great deal of controversy and led to the resignation of William Stainton Moses. However,

Hodgson and Mrs. Sidgwick were proven right when Eglinton was exposed as a fraud by other researchers. This was not a good start; stronger evidence was needed.

SOME CASES BACKED BY ROBUST EVIDENCE

In 1894 robust evidence appears to have been found. F. W. H. Myers and physicist Sir Oliver Lodge, another eminent member of the British SPR, had been invited by French physiologist Professor Charles Richet to attend a series of séances at his summer retreat on the Mediterranean island of Roubaud. They were invited to test the mediumistic skills of a rather uncouth Southern Italian woman called Eusapia Palladino. Palladino had already been investigated by the noted Italian psychiatrist Cesar Lombroso, who was convinced that she was genuine.

Palladino had been caught cheating in the past, usually after using crude props or with the assistance of an accomplice. However, on an isolated island without any associates with her, she managed to prove, at least as far as the three researchers were concerned, that she was capable of producing genuine phenomena. Later they were joined by the Sidgwicks who were less impressed but nevertheless concluded that something of scientific significance was taking place. However, when the results were published in the SPR *Journal,* Hodgson was highly critical of the controls and protocols applied during the sessions.

In July 1895 an attempt was made to settle the issue once and for all. Palladino was invited to give a series of séances in Cambridge. Much to the delight of Hodgson and his supporters, she was caught cheating. However, some argued that impossible controls were placed upon her, leaving her little option but to attempt a series of deceptions. A further series of tests were arranged for Palladino in 1908 in Naples. During these eleven sittings a series of phenomena were observed and concluded to be genuine. In his book *Is There an Afterlife?* the late professor David Fontana, a respected British philosopher, presents a list of what was observed by the investigative team. What is interesting about this list is that none of the observed phenomena involve anything remotely to do with spirit communication. It consists of a list of physical manifestations, all of which could have been faked by using accomplices or props.[1]

However, by this time Hodgson's attention had been drawn to another medium who showed extreme promise. Leonora Piper was called by William James in 1890 a "white crow." By this he meant that she provided the evidence that was needed to prove that mediumship was a true phenomenon of communication with the dead. Her initial guide was called "Phinuit," a Frenchman who didn't seem to understand French. David Fontana explains this by the fact that Mrs. Piper herself did not speak French and that because of this Phinuit "could not therefore find French words in her entranced mind."[2] Mrs. Piper had a series of other "controls," all of which had various abilities and levels of knowledge of French. (A *control* is one who facilitates communication between a medium and the presumably deceased communicator.)

The ASPR had been studying Mrs. Piper for some years. Due to financial problems, at that time the ASPR had become a branch of the SPR, and the young skeptic Hodgson was keen to see for himself if the claims made regarding Mrs. Piper were true. His proposal was accepted, and Mrs. Piper was invited to London to be observed and evaluated.

Hodgson conducted an in-depth investigation in which more than fifty sitters were brought together, all of them complete strangers to Mrs. Piper. He took the utmost precautions to prevent Mrs. Piper from getting information on the sitters beforehand. They were introduced anonymously or under a pseudonym and entered the room only after Mrs. Piper had gone into a trance. They took places behind her. Yet Mrs. Piper came up with facts that they were sure she could not have known through ordinary experience. William James himself concluded that Mrs. Piper could not possibly have collected the information by natural means.

An especially robust case was that involving George Pellew, known to Mrs. Piper as George Pelham (or simply as GP). Pellew, a young Boston lawyer, was extremely skeptical of the possibility of an afterlife, yet he promised Hodgson that, if he should die first, he would do his best to communicate with him. Two years later, at the age of thirty-two, Pellew died in an accident in New York. Soon afterward Hodgson arranged a séance with Mrs. Piper. He brought with him a young man called John Hart, a close friend of Pellew's. During the séance "Dr. Phinuit" conveyed several personal messages to Hart, convincing him that this was, indeed, his friend communicating with him from beyond the grave. Such was Hart's amazement at the accuracy of these messages that he contacted Jim and Mary Howard, fellow friends of the deceased lawyer and a couple known for their skepticism regarding such postmortem communications. Three weeks later the Howards, using false names, attended another Piper séance. Very quickly Pellew himself seemed to take control of Mrs. Piper. Speaking through the medium, Pellew was recorded as saying: "Jim, is that you? Speak to me quick. I am not dead. Don't think me dead. I'm awfully glad to see you. Can't you see me? Don't you hear me? Give my love to my father and tell him I want to see him. I am happy to be here, and more so since I find I can communicate with you. I pity those people who can't speak."

Howard responded, speaking through Mrs. Piper: "What do you do, George? Where are you?" Pellew answered, "I am scarcely able to do anything yet. I am just awakened to the reality of life after death. It was like darkness. I could not distinguish anything at first. Darkest hours just before dawn, you know that, Jim. I was puzzled, confused. Shall have an occupation soon. Now I can see you, my friend. I can hear you speak. Your voice, Jim. I can distinguish with your accent and articulation, but it sounds like a big bass drum. Mine would sound to you like the faintest whisper." Howard: "Our conversation then is something like telephoning?" "Yes." Howard: "By long distance telephone." GP laughed. Howard: "Were you surprised to find yourself living?" GP: "Perfectly so. Greatly surprised. I did not believe in a future life."

Speaking through Mrs. Piper, GP subsequently recognized by name twenty-nine of the thirty sitters Hodgson had introduced, the exception being a young woman who was a child when Pellew met her. GP carried on a conversation with each, showing an intimate knowledge of his relationship with them. He never once greeted any of the 120 sitters whom he had not known in his life.

Hodgson knew that Mrs. Piper did not know Pellew while he was alive. It appeared nearly impossible that she could nevertheless have impersonated him so precisely that thirty people whom Pellew did know had no doubt that it was really the deceased Pellew who spoke to them.

By 1898 Hodgson had become a firm believer of the genuineness of Mrs. Piper's transmissions. He wrote that "at the present I cannot profess to have any doubt but that the chief 'communicators' to whom I have referred . . . are veritably the personalities that they claim to be, that they have survived the change we call death, and that they have directly communicated with us whom we call living, through Mrs. Piper's entranced organism."[3]

The Cross-Correspondences

Mrs. Piper was also involved in a series of experiments that became known as the "cross-correspondences." Between the years of 1888 and 1902 three founding members of the Society for Psychical Research had passed away. In 1888 Edmund Gurney died suddenly of a suspected asthma attack at the age of thirty-eight. Frederic Myers followed his friend on January 17, 1901, both to be joined by

Henry Sidgwick the following year. These were all a great loss to the SPR, but at the same time this offered an opportunity for direct communication between the two worlds. All three men had stated that when on the "other side" they would attempt communication and, in doing so, give scientific proof of the persistence of consciousness beyond the brain.

Myers, the author of the classic two-volume work *Human Personality and Its Survival of Bodily Death,* had devised the method of cross-correspondences. This consists of messages that are meaningless by themselves, but acquire significance when joined together. A given medium would receive one element of the potentially meaningful message, and that message not only went beyond the knowledge and information that was available to that medium (in Myers's case it involved rather obscure references to classical literature), but it made no sense by itself. However, several messages of this kind, received by mediums that were not in any known form of communication with each other, when combined—sometimes following considerable research by specialized scholars—formed a meaningful message.

A team of mediums was created to facilitate these communications. The group eventually consisted of Margaret Verrall and her daughter, Helen; Mrs. Holland; Mrs. Willett; Mrs. King; and Leonora Piper. These were pseudonyms designed to protect the true identities of these women. In fact "Mrs. Holland" was Alice McDonald Fleming, the sister of the famous writer Rudyard Kipling. "Mrs. King" was Dame Edith Lyttelton, a novelist and political activist, and Mrs. Willett was Winifred Coombe-Tennant, a member of the landed gentry. With the exception of Mrs. Piper, none of them were professional mediums.

The intention was to open up communication with the deceased SPR founders by using a form of mediumship known as automatism. This involved the medium holding a pen against a piece of paper and waiting for the pen to be moved by the spirits taking over. In this way written messages could be sent from the other side. Over a period of nearly thirty years a series of mediums transcribed over 2,000 examples of automatic writing that were claimed to have come directly from Myers, Sidgwick, and Gurney. These consisted of fragmentary classical and literary allusions, the kind of messages that would be typical of highly educated individuals of the time.

Shortly after Myers's death, messages that presumably came from him were received by mediums in various parts of the world. Myers was aware of the problem of credibility in regard to messages coming purportedly from deceased individuals and was at great pains to overcome all reasonable doubt regarding the authenticity of his own messages. It was not enough for him that the content of his messages should not be known to the mediums that wrote them out; he sought to ensure that they would not be known to anyone with whom the mediums could have been in contact. Even if the medium's contact with another living person was not direct and conscious, it could have been indirect and unconscious: the messages could have been communicated to the medium telepathically or by clairvoyance. It was to exclude even this clearly remote possibility that Myers invented the method of cross-correspondences. The level of credibility in the case of Myers is significant, because it is extremely unlikely that the mediums who received his partial, and in-themselves meaningless, messages would have invented the messages themselves. In addition, understanding their meaning even when they were combined called for a high level of specialized knowledge of classical literature.

Following a period of trial (apparently to test the method of cross-correspondences and establish the credibility of his messages), Frederic Myers began to dictate lengthy messages to amateur trance medium Geraldine Cummins. Miss Cummins did not know Myers while he was living—she was just a child when Myers died—nor had she any particular knowledge of classical literature. Yet the contents of messages dictated by Myers—subsequently published as *The*

Road to Immortality (London, 1932) and *Beyond Human Personality* (London, 1935)—were so authentic that they convinced Sir Lawrence Jones, past president of the SPR and a close friend of the living Myers, that they came from Myers. And they so impressed Sir Oliver Lodge that he asked the discarnate Myers through Geraldine Cummins for permission to write a foreword to them. Mrs. Evelyn Myers, Frederic Myers's widow, was likewise fully convinced: she subsequently invited Miss Cummins to live with her in her own house.[4]

The Case of the Dead Poet

Another example of messages conveyed using the method of cross-correspondences involved the poet Roden Noel. On March 7, 1906, Mrs. Verrall began a session of automatic writing. The words "Tintagel and the sea that moaned in pain" appeared on the page. This meant absolutely nothing to Mrs. Verrall. She showed it to an SPR associate, Miss Johnson, who recognized it as being similar to the poem *Tintagel* by West Country poet Roden Noel.

Four days later "Mrs. Holland" received a similarly sourced automatic message. This read, "This is for A. W. Ask him what the date May 26, 1894, meant to him—to me—and to F. W. H. M. I do not think they will find it hard to recall, but if so—let them ask Nora." Not knowing what this meant, "Mrs. Holland" sent a message to the SPR in London.

On checking, it was discovered that "A. W." referred to Helen Verrall's husband, Dr. Verrall, and F. W. H. M. to Frederic Myers. "Nora" was Eleanor Sidgwick. All were good friends of the poet Roden Noel, the author of the poem associated with the message received by "Mrs. Holland" a few days previously. The date given was discovered to be the day that Roden Noel died.

On March 14 in Mrs. Holland's automatic writing appeared the words "Eighteen, fifteen, four, five, fourteen, fourteen, fifteen, five, twelve," and then the instruction to see the central eight words of

Revelations 13:18. Two weeks later, on March 28, Mrs. Holland wrote the words "Roden Noel," "Cornwall," "Patterson," and "do you remember the velvet jacket."

Another member of the team, Alice Johnson, then Honorary Secretary of the SPR, checked the central eight words of Revelations 13:18 and she found them to be "for it is the number of the man." Taking the clue at face value she went back to the numbers 18, 15, 4, 5, 14, 14, 15, 5, and 12 and substituted each number with the corresponding letter in the alphabet. This spelt Roden Noel. Subsequently Alice Jonson discovered that Noel used to regularly wear a velvet jacket, that "Cornwall" was the topic of several of his poems, and finally that A. J. Patterson was a mutual friend of his and Sidgwick's from their university days. None of this information had been known to any member of the group.[5]

This was but one of scores of cleverly devised puzzles created by the automatic writings generated in the cross-correspondences. The linked messages only made sense when understood in relation to the other messages received by unrelated individuals located in different parts of the country.

The Eileen Garrett Case

Another well-designed series of messages occurred later in 1930, received by a trance medium from somebody who had died two days earlier under tragic but spectacular circumstances. The recipient of the message was the Irish medium Eileen Garrett. Unlike many of her associates, Eileen accepted that her control, a being calling itself "Uvani," was simply an aspect of her own subconscious. In her autobiography *Many Voices* she made this opinion clear:

> I prefer to think of the controls as principals of the subconscious.
> I had, unconsciously, adopted them by name during the years of
> early training. I respect them, but cannot explain them.[6]

However, whatever the source of Eileen's information, it proved to be accurate, particularly in relation to her revelations regarding the crash of the R101 in 1930. On October 7, 1930, Garrett was at the National Laboratory of Psychical Research in West London. Her presence there had been set up by the psychic investigator, Harry Price, a man known for his dislike of fraudulent mediumship. In the presence of Price himself, Eileen was attempting to contact the spirit of the Scottish author Sir Arthur Conan Doyle, who had died earlier that year. However, Eileen's control Uvani was picking up other messages. In a classic "drop-in" case, Uvani announced the name "Irving" or "Irwin." Suddenly another voice broke in and gave a series of short, sharp statements. These consisted of phrases such as "the bulk of the airship was too heavy for her engines," "the mixture of carbon and hydrogen as fuel was absolutely wrong," and "the craft could not be trimmed, and nearly scraped the roofs at Achy."

Two days before, on October 5, 1930, the British airship R101 had crashed in a field in northern France and erupted in flames. Nearly everybody on board was killed. One of these was the pilot, Flight Lieutenant H. Carmichael Irwin. Everybody in the séance was fully aware of the disaster, as it had been headlines in all the newspapers. However, a great deal of detail regarding the crash had not been divulged to the media. Price was interested to know of the exact location of "Achy," the place whose rooftops were mentioned in the message. He looked through a series of conventional atlases and maps and found nothing. He then tracked down a large-scale railway map of the area around Beauvais, and he found it. Achy was a tiny hamlet a few miles north of Beauvais. This impressed him. How had Eileen, or her subconscious control Uvani, come by this information? Furthermore, the amount of technical detail recorded during the séance was far beyond many engineers, let alone the knowledge of an averagely educated person such as Eileen.[7]

Many attempts have been made to discredit this information. In the early 1960s researcher Archie Jarman did an exhaustive review of the event and uncovered some interesting facts. For example, Eileen's knowledge of the village of Achy was not as inexplicable as it may first have seemed. As somebody who knew Eileen well, Jarman was aware she frequently traveled by automobile from Calais to Paris. Achy was located on the main road route between the port and the capital city. He suggested that Eileen was subliminally aware of this and decided to use this hamlet as her envisaged location of the crash site.[8] But there were scores of hamlets, villages, and towns located on that road. What was the chance of her picking the right one randomly?

The Case of Gladys Leonard

In the early years of the twentieth century another British medium, Gladys Leonard, had a series of successes with regard to communication with the dead. Gladys Osborne Leonard (1882–1968) developed mediumistic skills as a child. From a very early age she claimed to have experienced visions of a beautiful landscape, which she termed "Happy Valleys." This consisted of a bucolic landscape projected onto the walls around her. These seemed to be like moving pictures, glimpses of a three-dimensional world that existed just outside the perceptions of most people. These were similar to the descriptions of the upper astral world. After receiving a vision of her mother she decided to develop her mediumistic skills. She soon manifested her "spirit guide." This being identified itself with a long, unpronounceable name, which became shortened to that of "Feda." In March 1914 Gladys was instructed to start a life as a professional medium. She was informed that "something big and terrible is going to happen in your world." A few months later the First World War broke out.

One of the casualties of this disaster was Raymond Lodge, who was killed in action on September 17, 1915. Raymond was the son of Sir Oliver Lodge, who was involved in the investigations of Eusapia

Palladino on the French island of Roubaud. Lodge's wife had a sitting with Mrs. Leonard on September 25, and during this séance Raymond came through. He stated, "Tell Father I have met some friends of his." In this message he specifically mentioned Myers.

On December 3 Lodge joined Leonard for a sitting. The spirit of Raymond joined them and through Gladys described a photograph that had been taken of him and his fellow officers. He said that in the picture he was seated while the others were "raised up." He then added that the picture had been taken outdoors with a black background "with lines going down." Lodge found this extremely strange. On November 29 he had received a letter from a total stranger called Mrs. Cheves. Her son had been a medical officer of the same battalion as Raymond. She informed Lodge that she had six copies of a photograph of a group of officers. She thought he may like one of them and offered to send him a copy. Lodge wondered if his son's message through Gladys was linked in some way to this picture.

Four days later, on December 7, 1915, the picture arrived. It was exactly as the spirit of Raymond had described, even to the "lines going down."[9]

In some messages transmitted through mediums the deceased "transcommunicator" appears fully committed to communicating with the living world. One such case involved the tragic death of a young man called Edgar Vandy, transmitted by Gladys in collaboration with two other mediums.

In August 1933 Edgar Vandy, a London-based engineer, was on a car ride in the Sussex countryside with two friends, a Mr. N. Jameson and his sister. They decided to stop off at the country estate of Miss Jameson's employer. It had been a long, hot drive, and the two men were delighted to discover that the estate had a swimming pool. Jameson, in a curious anticipation of events, had brought with him a swimsuit. However, Edgar had not. Fortunately, Miss Jameson was able to loan him one, and the two men changed behind a bush in preparation for their swim. For reasons unknown, Edgar did not wait for his friend to finish changing but made his own way to the swimming pool. On arrival at the pool, Jamison saw Edgar floating face down in the water. He jumped in and grabbed Edgar, only to have him slip from his grasp and sink in the murky water.

Jameson left the pool and went in search of help. It is unclear where his sister was at this time, but it is clear that Edgar was left in the pool for some time. It was about an hour before Jameson returned with a doctor and the police. They eventually managed to locate Edgar in the water, and his lifeless body was pulled out. The doctor noted slight abrasions on Edgar's chin and his tongue had been bitten through. Later it was also found that there was less fluid in his lungs than would have been had he drowned. From this the subsequent inquiry decided that Edgar had dived into the pool and knocked himself unconscious. The coroner returned a verdict of "Death by Drowning by Misadventure."

This verdict did not satisfy Edgar's brothers, Harold and George. They knew that their brother was not a good swimmer and was not the kind of person that would dive headlong into a pool full of murky water. They also questioned why Jameson did not drag Edgar out of the water before going to find help. There was also the question of where the sister had been while the tragedy was unfolding.

The brothers knew that a standard approach would not work. It was clear that the owner of the property was not keen to have bad publicity and would not cooperate with further investigations. As a member of the Society for Psychical Research, George was aware of what was known as "proxy sittings." This was a process whereby a number of mediums were used to elicit information from a deceased person. At each sitting no details about the case were supplied. Indeed false names and addresses of those requesting the sittings were supplied to the mediums. In this way no accusations of "cold reading" or prior research could be leveled.

George wrote to his fellow SPR member Drayton Thomas asking if a set of proxy sittings could be arranged. Thomas agreed to set it up. Thomas and the Vandy brothers had never met; the brothers said only that they were "trying to obtain more information about a brother who had died recently, and there were some doubts in the minds of relatives as to the cause of death."[10] Thomas got to work and decided that he would suggest Gladys together with three other mediums, Miss Campbell, Mrs. Mason, and Miss Bacon. At that time no report about Vandy's death had appeared in the London newspapers. However, a short report had appeared in the local press.

On September 6, 1933, Thomas attended one of his usual sittings with Gladys. He was there in a private capacity and was seeking information regarding his own family. Much to his surprise Leonard's control, Feda, announced, "Do you know a man who passed just lately; it was quite sudden?" Feda then mentioned two sets of initials, which fitted Edgar. It was Harold Vandy's initials that were mentioned by Feda, together with the initials of his recently deceased sister, Minnie. The control added, "This may be a proxy case about someone who went out through falling."[11] A stunned Thomas agreed that this unexpected message might refer to the case he had been asked to investigate. Feda then said that the case concerned somebody who was not a boy but was not old (Vandy was thirty-eight when the accident happened), and had met with a tragic end due to a fall. She added:

No one was at fault, he had had a funny feeling in his head, which he had had before . . . stepping out unconsciously . . . thinking of other things . . . I was holding, grasping something. Think I let go . . . Then it seemed as if my mind went curiously blank . . . I cannot remember exactly what happened—though I was falling down through something, as one does in sleep . . . It had nothing to do with them at all, and they could not

have helped me in any way at all . . . I'm so deeply sorry about
all the trouble.[12]

Thomas was stunned by this message, as he had not been thinking about Vandy at that time. He quickly wrote to the Vandy brothers
explaining what had taken place. A further five sittings were arranged,
using the mediums suggested by Thomas. At least one of the brothers was present at all of these sittings. But they did not identify themselves nor did they help the medium by asking leading questions or
making comments.

The sittings produced some accurate pieces of information.
For example, during the sitting of September 24, 1933, involving
Miss Campbell, the medium described how she could see Vandy's
"brother" showing himself to her holding a tennis racquet, adding
as an aside "which is odd as he didn't play tennis. He doesn't look
like a fellow who plays tennis." Prior to this, Campbell had informed
George Vandy, who at no time identified himself or gave any information about Edgar, that "You have a brother in the spirit world who died
as a result of an accident."

The tennis racquet made no sense to George. He had the short-
hand taker who was present (for this particular session he was "N.J.,"
the friend that was with Vandy the day he died) make a note that this
should be followed up. This they did and made a surprising discovery. A few weeks before his death Edgar and his sister were in the
garden at their home. The sister had a spare spool of film, and she
decided to use this to take a photograph of her brother. On that day
Edgar was wearing a tennis shirt, tennis trousers, and tennis shoes.
To complete the image they needed a tennis racquet. Edgar's sister
fetched her own racquet and asked him to pose with it. She recalled
that at the time he joked that people may be fooled into thinking he
was a tennis player.

Miss Campbell then said that Edgar was showing her a small gap in his teeth, "as if a tooth was missing," adding "Now he shows me an old scar and says 'That's my identification mark!'" On questioning, Campbell confirmed that the scar was on Edgar's face. George confirmed that Edgar had a small gap in his upper jawline where a tooth had broken off. He also had a large scar on his forehead. But what impressed George was his recollection that Edgar had once pointed at the scar and said "this will always identify me."

A few months later, on July 27, 1934, another "proxy" sitting took place that involved Gladys Leonard and Drayton Thomas. According to David Fontana, Mrs. Leonard was given no details regarding the reason for the sitting. It seems that Thomas's father began to communicate through Mrs. Leonard, stating that "the young man had a lot of papers he kept in a flat book form . . . one of them with writings and drawings. . . . Some brown . . . some almost like black covers." More than thirty years later George found these notebooks at a Pickfords' storage facility. In all twelve were found. Eleven had black covers, and one was brown.[13]

Channeled Messages in Criminal Cases

In February 1983 a twenty-five-year-old woman, Jacqueline Poole, was brutally murdered in her flat in Ruislip, North West London. The alarm was raised by her boyfriend's father, who was concerned that she had not been seen for two days. On breaking in, the police discovered Jacqueline's body and that a great deal of jewelry had been stolen. Fifteen months later the case was closed with the police unable to solve the crime.

In 1999 advances in forensic science brought about a reopening of the case. The police had obtained from the murder scene a small amount of DNA. This was subjected to a new technique known as "Low Copy Number" (LCN). These were matched to the DNA of one of the original suspects, Anthony James Ruark. In August 2001 Anthony Ruark was found guilty of Poole's murder and given a life sentence.

The backdrop to the successful prosecution involved a communication from a local medium, Christine Holohan, which had taken place in 1983. She had called the police in response to a television appeal for information about the Poole murder. Two police officers, Police Constable Tony Batters and Detective Constable Andrew Smith, had visited Mrs. Holohan the following day. Initially the officers had been suspicious, when Christine explained that she had been sensing a spirit around her, a spirit that she was sure was associated in some way with the murder. However, the spirit communicated to Christine that her name was Jacqui Hunt, not Jacqui Poole. This was of interest to the police officers, since they knew that the murdered woman's maiden name was Hunt.

Holohan then provided the police with no less than 131 separate facts about the murder. More than 120 of them were found to be correct. These included information that Jacqui's disembodied consciousness could have only seen after she had died; for example, that when the police made their forced entry there were two coffee cups in the kitchen. One was clean, and the other had the remains of coffee in the bottom. Holohan could not have known this. She also described that Jacqui had let her murderer into her flat, a man that she knew but did not like, and that earlier in the day two men had turned up at the flat to take her to work but she did not go with them because she felt ill. Holohan then described the murder in great detail, describing how rings had been taken off the body after death. She named a group of individuals known to Jacqui: one of them was somebody called "Tony." She added that she had tried automatic writing to get more details of the murderer, and her hand scrawled the name "Pokie." Another name she supplied was "Barbara Stone."[14]

The name "Pokie" caught the officers' attention. One of their initial key suspects had been Tony Ruark, a man who had the unusual nickname "Pokie." Based on Holohan's evidence Ruark was questioned and his home was searched. But no incriminating evidence was found, and he was released without charge. The police kept the pullover that was found in his dustbin. In the subsequent 1999 investigation samples of skin and bodily fluids added more DNA evidence to the minute traces of DNA found at the murder scene. Had Christine Holohan not contacted the police this search of Ruark's home would not have taken place and key evidence would not have been uncovered. Subsequently it was discovered that Barbara Stone was a good friend of Jacqui Poole who had died some years previously.

The Cases of Indridi Indridason

A remarkable case of medium-conveyed "news" was reported by Professor Erlendur Haraldsson at a lecture given to the Society for Psychical research on June 17, 2010. In this he discussed the work of the Icelandic medium Indridi Indridason.[15]

Indridason was born in October 1883 in Skardsstrond in northwestern Iceland. In the late nineteenth century this was a totally isolated community. There were no roads, just horse tracks. It would take at least three days on horseback to get from Skardsstrond to the capital, Reykjavik. At the age of twenty-two Indridason made this arduous journey to become a printer's apprentice. While in Reykjavik he stayed with relatives of his, the Einarssons. Indridi Einarsson and his wife had recently joined a spiritualist circle and one evening invited the young Indridason along. It was quickly discovered that Indridason had powerful mediumistic skills. There were reports of him levitating into the air while in communication with his controls. Indridason's primary control was his deceased great-uncle, Konrad Gislason, a professor of Nordic literature at Copenhagen University who had died in 1891. However, it was later recorded that twenty-six other spirits had spoken through him.

Indridason soon became a very popular medium, and his fame spread throughout Reykjavik. A group calling itself the Experimental

Society was set up solely to investigate Indridason's mediumistic abilities. It was thus under fairly controlled conditions that the séance of November 24, 1905, took place. That evening, at around nine, a new entity manifested itself. Through the mouth of the deeply entranced Indridason words in Danish began to be uttered. The words were delivered in a clear Copenhagen accent. This was surprising to all the Icelandic speakers present. At that time Iceland was part of Denmark, and Danish was spoken by many educated people. However, Indridason had received an extremely rudimentary education and spoke only a few words of Danish in, of course, an Icelandic, not a Copenhagen, accent. The voice introduced itself as being a "Mr. Jensen," a very common Danish surname. Jensen informed the stunned meeting that he had just joined them from Copenhagen, where he had witnessed a huge fire in a factory. The voice then disappeared only to reappear about an hour later to announce that the firemen had managed to bring the fire under control. He added that he was interested in this fire as he had been, in life, a "fabricant" (manufacturer).

According to the Minute Books of the Experimental Society, Jensen manifested again through the physical mediumship of Indridi Indridason. On December 11, 1905, he again spoke through Indridason and gave some further details about himself. He informed the group that his Christian name was Emil, that he was a bachelor with no children, and that he was "not so young" when he died. He added that he had siblings but they were "not here in heaven."[16]

It is important to stress that in 1905 there were no forms of communication between Iceland and Denmark other than by sea. In the winter this 1,300-mile sea voyage could take weeks. After the séance, it was not until Christmas that the first boat arrived. It carried, among many things, newspapers. An associate of the Experimental Society, the Right Reverend Hallgrimr Sveinsson, checked the Danish paper *Politiken*. An article described how a fire at a lamp factory at 63 Kongensgade in Copenhagen had broken out on the evening of November 24, adding that the conflagration was finally brought under control at around mid-night. Copenhagen is two hours ahead of Reykjavik, making the time of the ending of the fire to be around 10 p.m. Icelandic time, exactly the time that Jensen reappeared to give his news update.

In his research, subsequently described in a paper published in the SPR "Proceedings" in October 2011, Haraldsson found the report in the Saturday, November 25, 1905, edition of *Politiken*. This confirmed the details of the fire.

Haraldsson then checked through back copies of the news-paper to see how many fires had been reported in Copenhagen. He took a sample of the two weeks before the fire and the two weeks afterward. He discovered three minor fires, all of which were brought under control quickly. Two started in the early evening and one in the late morning. No fires matching the late evening timing were reported. Furthermore, there was only the one factory fire, the one at Kongensgade on the night of November 24.

Haraldsson was interested to discover if anybody with the name Emil Jensen had been living in Copenhagen in the years preceding the Kongensgade fire. In June 2009 he spent a day in Copenhagen going through the records in the Royal Library. There he found a list of professional people who lived and worked in the city. In the entry for 1890 he found Emil Jensen, who was recorded as a manufac-turer. Emil Jensen lived at Store Kongensgade 67, two doors away from number 63, the location of the 1905 fire. Following up this lead, Haraldsson discovered that Emil Jensen died on the third of August, 1898, at the age of fifty. He was unmarried and had no children. He had four sisters and two brothers, all of whom were still alive in 1905 when the "drop-in" took place.

In his summing up Haraldsson stated that:

The Jensen/Indridason case not only offers a strikingly convincing evidence for remote extrasensory perception—to use Rhine's terminology—but the motivational factor offers an intriguing argument for Emil Jensen being an independent entity distinct from the person of Indridi Indridason. [17]

Chess Game with a Deceased Grandmaster

Communicators, it seems, can not only dictate messages through automatic writing to trance mediums but can also engage in two-way interaction through the mediums. Brilliant evidence of this remarkable feature of medium-based communication was furnished by a game of chess between a living grandmaster and an entity who identified himself as a former chess grandmaster.

There is no known way the medium who channeled this game could have obtained the information that came from the deceased grandmaster: the medium himself did not play chess and claimed to have little or no interest in the game. Yet the messages conveyed by him were not only extremely expert in regard to that game but also pointed specifically to the style of the deceased grandmaster. The case was the following.

Wolfgang Eisenbeiss, an amateur chess player, engaged the medium Robert Rollans to transmit the moves of a game played by the living Viktor Korchnoi, then the world's third-ranked grand-master, with a player whom Rollans was to find in his state of trance. Eisenbeiss gave Rollins a list of deceased grandmasters and requested Rollins to enter the state of trance and ask who among the deceased grandmasters would be willing to play. On June 15, 1985, the former Hungarian grandmaster Geza Maroczy responded.

Maroczy was the third-ranking grandmaster in the year 1900. Rollans transmitted the reason given by Maroczy: "I will be at your disposal in this peculiar game of chess for two reasons. First, because I also want to do something to aid mankind living on Earth to become convinced that death does not end everything, but instead the mind is separated from the physical body and comes up to us in a new world, where individual life continues to manifest itself in a new unknown dimension. Second, being a Hungarian patriot, I want to guide the eyes of the world into the direction of my beloved Hungary."[18]

Korchnoi and Maroczy began to play. It was a protracted game due to Korchnoi's illness and his frequent travels: it lasted no less than seven years and eight months. Speaking through Rollans, who in his normal state of consciousness would not have had any idea of what was going on, Maroczy gave his moves in the standard form known to chess players—for example, "5. A3 – Bxc3+"—and Korchnoi replied to Rollans in the same form. Every move has been recorded. The game ended on February 11, 1993, when at move forty-eight, Maroczy resigned. Subsequent analysis showed that it was a wise move: five moves later, Korchnoi would have achieved checkmate.[19]

Cases of Group-Conveyed Communications

A recurring element of medium-transmitted communication is the facilitation of the communication by a group of mediums working together. Among the first to remark on this kind of "spirit-collaboration" was the medium William Stainton Moses.

William Stainton Moses, who was born in 1839, was ordained as an Anglican priest in 1870, but after attending his first séance in 1872, he became fascinated by the experiences transmitted by mediums. He discovered that he had mediumship skills himself and devoted his energies to exploring them. He was responsible for the establishment of the British National Association of Spiritualists in 1873. In 1882 he was also involved in the creation of the SPR. This association was not to last long. As we have already discussed, he resigned from the SPR after Richard Hodgson's dismissal of the claims of William Eglinton in the SPR *Journal*.

Moses's mediumship involved the use of passive, or automatic, writing, exactly the same process used during the cross-correspondences. He started receiving messages in this way in March 1873. Each section of automatic writing would be signed, "Doctor, the Teacher." Soon more spirits came through, but eventually one spirit communicated on behalf of the rest. It identified itself as "Rector." A second group, headed by an entity calling itself "Imperator," soon appeared. A transcript recorded by Dr. Speer, a member of Moses's group, includes the following statement:

> I, myself, Imperator Servus Dei, am the chief of a band of forty-nine spirits, the presiding and controlling spirit, under whose guidance and direction the others work . . . I am come from the seventh sphere to work out the will of the Almighty; and, when my work is complete, I shall return to those spheres of bliss from which none returns again to earth. But this will not be till the medium's work on earth is finished, and his mission on earth exchanged for a wider one in the spheres.

Imperator then explained that both "Rector" and the "Doctor" were part of his team. Rector was his deputy and lieutenant, and the role of the Doctor was to guide the pen of the receiving medium. Imperator, and occasionally Rector, would dictate information to the Doctor, who would then guide the hand of the medium. In this way messages were transferred from the "seventh sphere" to Earth. Also involved in the team of four were beings called "Guardians." The team consisted of seven entities. They were part of a much larger group that they said was responsible for guiding life on Earth.[20]

The communications of the group were investigated by F. W. H. Myers. He reported in the *Proceedings* of the SPR that the communications:

were not produced fraudulently by Dr. Speer or other sitters. . . .
I regard as proved both by moral considerations and by the fact
that they were constantly reported as occurring when Mr. Moses
was alone. That Mr. Moses should have himself fraudulently produced them I regard as both morally and physically incredible.
That he should have prepared and produced them in a state of
trance I regard both as physically incredible and also as entirely
inconsistent with the tenor both of his own reports and those of
his friends. I therefore regard the reported phenomena as having
actually occurred in a genuinely supernormal manner.[21]

MEDIUM-TRANSMITTED COMMUNICATION: WHAT THE EVIDENCE TELLS US

As already remarked, medium-transmitted communication with
deceased persons is subject to doubt. Is it truly communication with
deceased persons transmitted by the mediums, or is it produced in
some way by the mediums themselves?

The cases reviewed here offer reasonable evidence that the
mediums did not invent the messages themselves because they did
not possess the information contained in the messages. In some cases
a language unknown to them was used, and in others skills and
knowledge were involved (as in the case of the chess game between
the living and the deceased grand masters) that the mediums themselves did not possess.

Could the mediums have picked up the information they channeled in some hidden or unusual way from living persons? As far as
could be ascertained, in the above cases nobody in the environment of
the mediums had the pertinent information. Could the mediums have
picked up the information from persons beyond their own environment? This would suggest that they could scan the field of relevant

knowledge and receive the information they wanted through a form of super-ESP. This possibility cannot be excluded, but it calls for a kind of process that is hardly more credible than communication with the dead. But the super-ESP hypothesis is placed in question by the game with the deceased chess grandmaster. It is not likely that there would have been any currently living person who had the knowledge shown in this game: knowledge not only of chess at the grandmaster level but knowledge of the particular style of the grandmaster who died over a hundred years ago and dictated the moves in the game.

In the above cases the messages conveyed by the mediums seem to have originated with an entity that had information that neither the mediums themselves nor anyone they could access is likely to have possessed. Just as remarkably, in some cases the communicating entity displayed the intention to communicate, whether to clear up an unsolved crime or to shed light on a hitherto unknown event. It also displayed the intention to dispel all reasonable doubt regarding the authenticity of its messages. In these cases fraud, whether conscious or unconscious, seems nearly excluded. It appears that the contacted entity is a quasi-living consciousness that is not the consciousness of a presently living person.

4

INSTRUMENTAL
TRANSCOMMUNICATION*

According to experience with "Electronic Voice Phenomena" (EVP), contact and communication with deceased persons—known as "transcommunication"—can also be created electronically. EVP is a repeatedly observed phenomenon, which recently has also been recorded. A number of books and articles have been published protocolling the relevant observations and experiments.

The EVP experimenter whose work first attracted wide international attention was the Latvian Konstantin Raudive. In his 1971 book *Breakthrough* he reported that he had recorded some 72,000 voices emitted by unexplained paranormal sources, of which 25,000 contained identifiable words. Since then a wide range of controlled experiments have been carried out.

Research on EVP is spreading; the number of serious investigators is increasing. One of the most respected researchers in the field is François Brune, a Catholic priest who has been surveying the field

---

*The authors wish to thank Dr. Anabela Cardoso, the world's foremost living authority on instrumental transcommunication, for her precious collaboration in drafting this chapter.

for many years and has written a series of books on this subject. Father Brune estimates that there are many thousands of researchers in various parts of the world, mainly concentrated in America and Europe.

EARLY EXPERIMENTS WITH ELECTRONICALLY TRANSMITTED COMMUNICATION

At the end of the nineteenth century scientists discovered that the physical world manifested to the senses is only one aspect of a complex universe filled with invisible rays, radiations, and fields. These discoveries encouraged the expectation that through these invisible regions or dimensions, contact and communication could be created with those who have "passed over"—conceivably into another dimension of the universe.

The idea that there is a world beyond the reach of our senses gained currency with a discovery made by German-born British physicist William Herschel. Herschel was measuring the temperatures of different colors by moving a thermometer through light split by a prism into a rainbow. He noticed that the highest temperature was beyond the red end of the spectrum, located where the rainbow had ended. The following year, in 1801, German chemist Johan Ritter noticed that at the other end of the rainbow another invisible form of light catalyzed chemical reactions. It was clear from these discoveries that visible light was only a part of a much broader, partly invisible, spectrum.

In 1845 Michael Faraday noted that when light traveled through a transparent material it was affected by a magnet. This became known as the "Faraday effect." In 1864 Scottish mathematician James Clerk Maxwell discovered that "electromagnetism" and light were the same phenomenon.

Maxwell subsequently developed a set of mathematical equations that predicted the behavior of these electromagnetic (EM) waves and suggested that there are an infinite number of frequencies that radiate throughout space.

In 1866 Heinrich Hertz used Maxwell's equations to discover another form of electromagnetic energy, called radio waves. They could be used to send messages wirelessly from one location to another at the speed of light. Telegraphy, using Morse code, had been sending wire-transmitted messages since the 1840s, but the wireless system using radio waves was revolutionary.

That radio waves were totally invisible to human beings was seen as evidence that—outside of everyday perceptions—the universe contained vast amounts of information that could be captured by man-made receivers. Sir Oliver Lodge, a physicist known for his development of electromagnetic theory, began experiments at the end of the nineteenth century. On August 14, 1894, at a meeting of the British Association for the Advancement of Science, he demonstrated the communication potential of radio signals. The preceding year Serbian scientist Nikola Tesla demonstrated the similar potential of Tesla waves, and a year later Guglielmo Marconi exhibited the electromagnetic field as an invisible communication medium. These scientists believed that this form of communication could also be used to communicate with higher planes of existence.

EM "spirit- or transcommunication" received a technical boost in 1877 when Edison discovered a process to record and replay human voices. Records could now be kept of human voices as well as of musical events.

In 1901 in Siberia the American ethnographer Waldemar Borogas was researching the customs of the Chukchee shamans. He used the portable Edison phonograph to record the chants and invocations of the shamans for later analysis. Borogas witnessed the ceremonies in which shamans enter their dream states; these ceremonies involve rhythmic drumbeats. Much to his surprise, as he was witnessing these ceremonies, he heard disembodied voices, which were also recorded by the phonograph.[1] In his book *Talking to the Dead* George Noory wrote that at a later session the shamans communicated directly with the source of the voices, and they obliged by again manifesting the voices and letting them be recorded.[2] Unfortunately these priceless recordings have been lost.

Another device that has been lost is the "Cambraia Vocative Telephone" invented by Brazilian-based Portuguese researcher Augusto de Oliveira. De Oliveira was not alone in his interest. In 1933 a fellow Brazilian, Prospero Lapagese, published plans for an "electric medium-istic device" that would not only capture spirit voices but would also photograph the communicators using a form of X-ray. It is not known whether this machine was ever built. But the Portuguese-Brazilian Oscar d'Argonnel seems to have been the first to receive real telephone conversations from the deceased. In a little book in Portuguese called *Voices of the Beyond by the Telephone.* He described in detail how he had hundreds of clear conversations through the telephone with deceased friends and family members, as well as with some previously unknown personalities.[3] He obtained information from them that was unknown to everybody involved and was able to later confirm and ver-ify the authenticity of the information. Much of the information con-cerned the dimension where the deceased now exist. The descriptions of the characteristics of these extraordinary contacts perfectly match the voices received by other ITC researchers years later, as well as the information provided by them.

SOME CASES OF
INSTRUMENTAL TRANSCOMMUNICATION

The various forms of Instrumental Transcommunication (ITC) include radios, TVs, telephones, computers, cameras, and other technical devices.

Cases of Voice-Transcommunication

In the 1930s and 1940s interest diminished in electronic transcom-munication, and the subject was forgotten about until September

1952, when two Catholic priests heard something strange on their tape recordings.

Father Agostino Gemelli and Father Pellegrino Ernetti were in the process of recording Gregorian chants at the Laboratory of Physics at the Catholic University of Milan. Much to the frustration of Gemelli, the wire tapes kept breaking. As was his habit when frustrated, he called out to his dead father for assistance. This was simply a way of letting off steam, probably the sacerdotal version of swearing. After a few minutes of manipulation the tape was repaired. The priests then played back the recording. Much to their surprise there was no evidence of any Gregorian chanting; there was only a voice saying, "Of course I can help you; I am always with you." Gemelli immediately recognized the voice to be that of his father. Astounded, the priest decided to repeat the recording. This time Gemelli asked, "Is it really you, Papa?" With mounting excitement the priests played back the tape. "Of course it is I; don't you recognize me, *testone*?" *Testone* is an Italian term of endearment equivalent to the English "thickhead."

The fathers were both delighted and concerned. They decided to discuss this with the pope himself, Pius X. Much to their relief Pius told them that this could be "the beginning of a new scientific study that would confirm faith in the Beyond."[4]

In 1969, as a token of gratitude for his work at the Vatican, where he painted several portraits of the pope, and for his documentary *The Fisherman from Galilee—On the Grave and Stool of Peter,* Pope Paul VI awarded the Ukrainian-born Swede Friedrich Jürgenson the Commander Cross of the Order of St. Gregory the Great, one of the five orders of Knighthood of the Holy See. Jürgenson was one of the most influential ITC researchers of his time, as well as a renowned painter, musician, and film director. He had first encountered the phenomenon in 1959 while recording birdsong near his home in Mölnbo in Sweden. When he played back the recording he was surprised to hear a man's voice on the tape. He was speaking in Norwegian and discussing the nocturnal habits of birds. It was this coincidence that led Jürgenson to believe that this was not a simple stray radio broadcast picked up by his recorder.

A few weeks later he captured another voice. This time it was female and seemed to be addressing him directly. It asked, "Friedel, my little Friedel, can you hear me?" Friedel was the pet name used by his deceased mother, who had died years before. This convinced Jürgenson that these communications were from sentient individuals who had passed over. His mother spoke to him in German, and the original recording was in Norwegian. Over the years he captured many recordings in a large number of languages, and many of them were subsequently identified as deceased family members or close friends.[5]

In 1964 Jürgenson published his book *The Voices from Space*. This brought about a long research relationship with Professor Hans Bender, director of the Institute of Parapsychology at the University of Freiburg. Bender worked with Jürgenson at various locations across the world and used many different types of recording equipment. Although he considered the phenomenon to be genuine, Bender was basically antagonistic to the idea and did not accept the recordings to be evidence of the survival of consciousness after death. Instead he suspected that Jürgenson's own subconscious influenced the recordings psychokinetically.[6]

Perhaps the most important researcher to subsequently enter this field was Konstantin Raudive. Raudive had written a series of books after WWII, focusing on what may happen to consciousness after the death of the body. In the early 1960s, when he came across the work of Jürgenson, Raudive was living in West Germany. After meeting with Jürgenson he had set up his own research project and in 1968 published the results of his experiments under the title *Unhörbares Wird Hörbar*. This is the book mentioned earlier, published in the UK under the title *Breakthrough*.

One of the techniques used by Raudive was to tune a radio to a frequency where there was no transmission and record the resulting static hiss on tape. Raudive claimed that sometimes voices could be heard speaking within this "white noise." On various occasions he received messages that were personal to him, many in Latvian. A great number of them stated that they came from his deceased friends and family members. He also noticed that the voices seemed to speak at more than twice the speed of regular human discourse. He minutely identified other peculiar characteristics enumerated in his book. In spite of accusations by researchers not familiar with the languages spoken by the voices that some of his recordings were snatches of conversations that made little sense, the great majority of his messages were precise and pertinent. His book *Breakthrough*, which contains the transcription of thousands of messages in over 240 pages, testifies to the relevance of his messages to researchers, to participants in ITC experiments, and to all observers of the phenomena.[7]

Jürgenson and Raudive worked together on various occasions, and each time their respective results were confirmed. For example, in 1967 Jürgenson claimed that he could understand all of the three hundred or so voices that Raudive had recorded over the years. He suggested that some of the voices on his own recordings were the same as those recorded by Raudive.

Just before Raudive's book *Breakthrough* was published in 1971, the English publisher Colin Smythe set up a series of experiments involving technicians from Pye Recording Studios. Four reel-to-reel tape recorders were shielded from all possible radio interference and left to play for eighteen minutes. Much to the surprise of the technicians, the tapes registered sounds even though nothing was heard through the monitoring headphones. When the tapes were played back, more than two hundred separate voices were heard, twenty-seven of which made clearly understandable statements. According to Peter Bander, one of the witnesses, Sir Robert Mayer, was convinced that one of the voices was that of his recently deceased friend, pianist Arthur Schnabel.[8]

A second series of experiments took place at the Enfield studios of Belling and Lee. Again a series of clear EVP voices were recorded, notwithstanding extensive shielding for stray radio transmissions. In the same year recently retired engineer, inventor, and businessman George Meek opened a small laboratory in Philadelphia. Meek was a wealthy man who had been fascinated by paranormal phenomena during most of his life. His main interest was in EVP, and he believed that the anomalous voices could only be analyzed in detail if the equipment was updated. He felt that the knowledge of how to do this was not available on this side of the communication channel and that he needed to elicit the help of a scientist or engineer that had "passed over." He was well aware that, in general, communication with the dead was facilitated by a medium. He therefore placed an ad in the magazine *Psychic Observer*. He was extremely fortunate that this ad was seen by a gifted clairvoyant, William O'Neil. Unusually for individuals of this calling, O'Neil was also a keen amateur electrical engineer. He was therefore in the unique position of being able to understand any technical instructions that he might receive from a deceased engineer who would wish to become involved in this ambitious project. In 1973 O'Neil was placed on Meek's payroll, and the search for a suitably qualified contact on the other side began.

Within a few weeks contact was made by a disincarnate entity that identified itself as Dr. George Mueller. Keen to prove that this entity was what he claimed to be, Meek, through O'Neil, asked for details of Mueller's life. These were quickly supplied and proved to be accurate. Through the details the investigators were able to trace the life of the real Dr. George Mueller. The entity described that in life he had graduated with a BS in electrical engineering in 1928. This was awarded by the University of Wisconsin at Madison, and Mueller graduated in the top 20 percent of his class. He then went on to earn an MS at Cornell in 1930, followed by a PhD at the same institution. Of course all this information could have been discovered by O'Neil himself. However, there were other elements that were less easy to discover. Through O'Neil the deceased Mueller also gave his social security number, but—of even more significance—he described in detail the machine he had invented for the treatment of arthritis. This information was not in the public domain; indeed, it was only known to Mueller himself. Meek's team subsequently built a prototype following the instructions of the deceased scientist, and it worked effectively.

The small team of Meek, O'Neil, and their spirit associate worked together on the design and construction of a machine that became known as the "Spiricom." Such was Meek's enthusiasm for this communication tool that he set up the MetaScience Foundation in North Carolina and invested over half a million dollars in its development. Meek announced to the world in 1982 that a powerful communication device had been perfected that would allow two-way communication between this world and the world of spirit.

Sadly, the success of Spiricom was to be soon curtailed. The team's contact on the other side, George Mueller, had long warned that he would not be around to facilitate communications for long. He worked with O'Neil and Meek to try to find ways of building a more powerful communication device, but time was running out. Contact was soon lost, and the Spiricom fell silent. Meek continued his work and lectured around the world, advocating that genuine, direct contact can be made with the dead. As has happened in other impressive cases of electronic transcommunication, accusations of fraud leveled against the Spiricom soon started to surface. However, Meek's books and John Fuller's minute description of his in-loco[9] observations of the work of both George Meek and O'Neil make clear their authenticity.[10]

The influence of Jürgenson then stimulated Hans Otto König, a professional electroacoustics engineer, to enter the field. One evening in 1974, as König was watching TV at his home in the city of Mönchengladbach, he saw a program featuring Friedrich Jürgenson and Hans Bender speaking on EVP. Whereas the show's overall tone was skeptical, König decided to start his own experiments. He suspected that the voices emanated from the subconscious mind of the experimenter rather than from the dead. Initially he used the standard method of tuning his radio to a frequency where only static could be heard. However, he heard the voice of his deceased mother addressing him by name and asking if she could be heard. This convinced him that the voices were what Jürgenson believed them to be: communications from another dimension in space and time. He continued his experiments, using running water as a background noise. Over time he became convinced that the way to make the communication more effective was to use "white noise" in the frequency domain of ultrasound (above the audible range of 20 to 20,000 Hertz) that magnetic tape recorders can capture. As ultrasound was König's area of expertise, he was ideally positioned to test spirit communication in that range.

König soon developed equipment that facilitated two-way contact in a way similar to Meek's Spiricom. On November 6, 1982, at a symposium of the German EVP organization, the VTF (*Verein fuer Tonbandstimmenforschung*—Association for Research on Tape-Recorded Voices) he presented the fruits of his labor to the world: a device he called the *Ultraschallgenerator* (Ultrasonic Generator). This was witnessed by several hundred people. It seemed to work well in a series of communications heard by all those present.

On the evening of January 15, 1983, millions of people listened when he presented his system on a live radio broadcast called *Unglaubliche Geschichten* (Unbelievable Stories). Hosted by presenter Rainer Holbe, this was a popular broadcast over large areas in Northern Europe. The audience clearly heard a series of responses to questions from König to his supposed transdimensional "commu-nicators." In German he asked, "May I try to get in contact with you?" and received the reply: "*Versuch!*" (Try!). He then asked if the entities could hear him and if he had got the right frequency; he was told, "*Wir hören Deine Stimme*" (We hear your voice). Until this stage the status of the communicators was unclear.

However, in one intriguing, and seemingly unrelated, response, a communicator said, "*Otto König macht Totenfunk.*" This brought about a stunned reaction from all concerned. The word *Totenfunk* had been newly created by the researchers to describe radiophony with the dead. This showed that the communicators were in some way aware of information that had not been part of previous direct communications. It was considered significant that the communica-tors had identified König by name. In another exchange an entity stated, "*Ich komm nach Fulda*" (I come to Fulda). Fulda was the small German town where the November 1982 symposium took place. This suggested that the entities take note of where they are communicat-ing with the living.

As it has happened in other instances in a field of such contro-versial nature, the validity of Hans-Otto König's Ultrasonic Generator has been questioned.

More recently Dr. Anabela Cardoso, a Portuguese senior career diplomat, carried out a series of remarkable experiments. She used white noise from short wave radios and an AM radio tuned to around 1500 KHz as acoustic background. This frequency is known as the "wave" by EVP experimenters, as this is the frequency with which Jürgenson had the most success.[11]

Having received answers to her questions, both on tape and directly through the radio, Cardoso became convinced that the phe-nomena are authentic and merit documentation and exploration. She created the international periodical, the *ITC Journal,* to publish research reports initially in Portuguese, Spanish, and English. A few years later the *Journal* was published only in English. Cardoso's own communicators spoke mostly Portuguese, with occasional communications in Spanish and English, all languages in which she was fluent. According to David Fontana, who witnessed several of Cardoso's experiments, in these experiments the possibility of fraud or interference by other persons can be effectively ruled out.[12]

In 2010 Anabela Cardoso wrote a book about her ITC work and published a CD with samples of the anomalous electronic voices reported in her book.[13]

Sponsored by two international scientific foundations, a series of highly controlled experiments aimed at recording anomalous electronic voices were carried out in Vigo, Spain, during 2008 and 2009. Anabela Cardoso was the research director and the main operator of the EVP tests that assembled a team of renowned European ITC operators. The tests were inspired by Hans Bender's work with Jürgenson and by Konstantin Raudive's experiments in England, documented by Peter Bander, Colin Smythe's associate editor.[14]

A large number of experiments were carried out at the highly shielded Laboratory of Acoustics of the School of Engineering at Vigo University as well as at a professional recording studio during a period of two years. The tests were supervised by independent electronic engineers and sound technicians. A substantial number of positive results were obtained, as detailed in the report.[15]

Cases of Video-Transcommunication

In November 1982 a group of friends in Germany met with Klaus Schreiber, who suggested that they should try EVP themselves. He turned on a tape recorder and invited a dead friend to join them. They all sat in silence as the tape recorded the ambient sounds in the room. After ten minutes or so they switched the machine off and played back what had been recorded. Initially nothing was heard; then, as the tape came to an end, they all clearly heard the words "Hello, friends."

Schreiber was convinced that EVP provided a powerful tool for communication with the dead. He subsequently set up a series of recording devices in the basement of his house in the hope of catching anomalous communications. However, instead of using as background sound a radio tuned to a single bandwidth of "white noise," he used a device called "psychofon," invented by Viennese EVP researcher Franz Seidl. This device continually scanned an extensive area of bandwidth, producing a sound field qualitatively different from that of ordinary white noise. Schreiber claimed to have received many messages from the deceased using this setup.

It appears that the communicators wanted to develop the channels of communication into the video range. The initial EVP message received by Schreiber, purportedly from his daughter, stated, "We come via television" (*Wir kommen ueber Fernsehen*), followed by "Soon you (will) see us in television" (*Bald siehst du uns im Fernsehen*). In May 1984 the messages became more specific, carrying the instruction "Record this in TV" (*Spiel im TV ein*).

In response to these requests Schreiber set up a sophisticated electro-optical feedback loop with a video camera filming a television receiver tuned to a blank channel. The signal from the video camera was fed back to the TV monitor, which was then recorded by the video camera. The latter was placed at an angle slightly off-center in relation to the TV screen. The result was a series of light patterns, which Schreiber analyzed frame by frame.

In one of his early experiments Schreiber claims to have received an image of his dead daughter Karin. From then on Karin became his facilitator from the other side. Karin informed her father that the images could only be in black and white because her world had not yet developed the technology to broadcast images in color. Soon other images appeared as well, some of them of famous now-deceased German media personalities such as Romy Schneider and Kurt Juergens. The appearance on the TV screen of Romy Schneider was witnessed by the Radio Luxembourg presenter Rainer Holbe. It has been claimed that as she appeared her voice was recorded as saying, "My son is with me—we are all united here" (*Mein Sohn ist bei mir—wir alle sind hier vereint*).[16]

Schreiber died in 1988, but his work has been continued by his friend Martin Wenzel and by a Luxembourg-based couple, Maggy and Jules Harsch-Fischbach. On the first of July 1988, they received clear images and sounds apparently from another dimension. They were assisted by an entity that the Harsch-Fischbachs later called "The Technician." The Harsch-Fischbachs believed that the transmissions were facilitated by the deceased Konstantin Raudive. They were informed that the group they were working with was called Timestream.

Working closely with the Harsch-Fischbachs were the German researchers Friedrich Malkhoff and Adolf Homes. In the autumn of 1987, Malkhoff heard a radio broadcast about EVP directed by Rainer Holbe. He was intrigued and decided to attempt some recordings himself. Much to his surprise he found voices on his tapes. Soon, in the spring of 1988, he came across a magazine advertisement by Adolf Homes. Homes also lived in the Trier area and was looking for somebody who shared his interests in EVP. He received communication from an entity whose instructions were similar to those received from "The Technician." Malkhoff and Homes believed that they were in contact with the same entity.

In Luxembourg the Harsch-Fischbachs received messages that were allegedly from a group of historical personages, including the British explorer Richard Burton, French chemist Henri Sainte-Claire Deville, German rocket scientist Werner von Braun, and the Swiss occultist Paracelsus. Also in this group were entities claiming to be Raudive and Jürgenson and an entity that identified herself as Swejen Salter. She said that she had lived her physical life on a planet other than Earth.

On July 20, 1990, the German and the Luxembourg teams decided to join forces. A few days later the Harsch-Fischbachs received a message that said, "We, the group *Zeitstrom,* jointly with the group *Centrale.*" Apparently the communicators decided to follow the example of their earthly contacts in joining together. In communication with them, the teams on "this side" obtained the most impressive results ever achieved in the history of ITC. The information came through their computers, telephones, and a complicated audio equipment setup at the Harsch-Fischbachs' home under the guidance of "The Technician." A large number of messages were received from Konstantin Raudive, and there were a series of cross-correspondences similar to those inaugurated by Myers a few years earlier.

During one session Raudive introduced to the living Luxembourg group a new member of the *Zeitstrom* team called Carlos de Almeida. Almeida spoke to the Harsch-Fischbachs in Portuguese. He called the *Zeitstrom* team in Portuguese "Rio do Tempo." (In English *zeit-strom* is "Timestream.") Having been told about this happening by a Portuguese acquaintance of the Harsch-Fischbachs who came to visit her, Anabela Cardoso decided to ask her fellow Portuguese speaker Carlos de Almeida for assistance in her transcommunication experiments. Soon she was in regular communication with him and other members of the Rio do Tempo group.[17]

There are cases of instrumental transcommunication in which reasonable doubt is nearly excluded. Both authors of this study experienced such cases, and Laszlo reported on one of them in his book *Quantum Shift in the Global Brain.* The following paragraphs, excerpted from that book, describe the experiment.

April 7, 2007. I am sitting in a darkened room in the Italian town of Grosseto, together with a group of sixty-two other people. It is evening, and there is not a sound, other than the sounds of the shortwave band of a radio. It is an ancient valve radio, the kind that works not with transistors, but with vacuum tubes. I am sitting on a small stool immediately behind an old Italian who wears a hat and is dressed as if it were still winter, although it is warm in the room—and getting warmer by the minute.

The Italian—a renowned psychic who considers himself not a commercial medium but a serious psychic researcher— is Marcello Bacci. For the past forty years he has been hearing voices through his radio, and has become convinced that they are the voices of people who have passed away. Those who come to his regular "dialogues with the dead" are likewise convinced of this. They are people who have lost a son or a daughter, a father or a mother or a spouse, and hope to have the experience of hearing them talk through Bacci's radio.

We have been sitting in the darkened room for a full hour. Bacci is touching the wooden box that houses the radio with both hands, caressing it on the sides, at the bottom and on the top, and speaking to it. "Friends, come, speak to me, don't hesitate, we are here, waiting for you . . ." But nothing happens. As Bacci plays with the dial, the radio emits either the typical shortwave static, or conveys one or another shortwave broadcast. I am getting convinced that the doubts I had initially entertained were justified: after all, how could a shortwave receiver pick up voices from the "other side"? How could the "other side" transmit signals through the electromagnetic spectrum? Bacci keeps caressing the radio, turning the dial, and asking for the voices. I sit behind him, and wait for a miracle . . .

And then: there are sounds like heavy breathing, or like a rubber tube or pillow pumped with air. Bacci says: "At last!" He continues to move the dial, but there are no longer any shortwave transmissions coming through. Wherever he turns the dial, the radio transmits only the periodic breathing. The entire radio seems to have become tuned to this one frequency, one that an associate of Bacci is carefully monitoring on a device to my right.

Bacci talks to the radio, encouraging whoever or whatever is breathing, or pumping air, to talk back to him. Now voices are coming through on the air. Indistinct, hardly human voices, difficult to understand, but they speak Italian, and Bacci seems to understand. The entire room freezes in concentration. The first voice is that of a man. Bacci talks to him, and the voice answers. Bacci tells him that there are many people here tonight (the usual group is no more than twelve), and they are all anxious to get into a conversation.

Bacci says that behind him—immediately to my left—sits someone whom they know. "Who is he?" He is the renowned French psychic-researcher Father Brune. He lost his brother about a year ago and has contacted him since, and hopes to do so again. The voice answers, "Père Brune" (as Fr. Brune is known in his native France). Fr. Brune asks, "With whom am I speaking?" It turns out that it is not his brother, but Father Ernetti, the priest who was involved in the original experiments. He was a close friend and associate of Fr. Brune who died not long ago.

They talk for a while, and then Bacci—who continues to lean forward and caress the radio—says, "Do you know who else is sitting here, just behind me?" A voice that seems to be different, but also male, says "Ervin." He pronounces it as one does in Hungarian or in German, with the "E" as in "extraordinary" and not, as in English, as in "earth." Bacci asks, "Do you know who he is?" and the voice answers, "*É ungherese*" (He is Hungarian). The voice then gives my family name, but pronounces it as Italians sometimes do: "Latzlo," and not as Hungarians, with a soft "s" as in "Lasslo."

Bacci asks for my hand—I am sitting immediately behind

him—and places my hand on his. His wife and long-standing associate places her hand on mine. My hand is sandwiched between theirs, and is getting warmer—indeed, quite hot. Bacci tells me, "Speak to them in Hungarian." I lean forward and do so. My voice is choked, for I am moved. The unthinkable is happening, just as I hoped but hardly dared to expect. I say how happy I am to speak with them. I do not think I should ask whether they are dead (how do you say to someone you talk to, "Are you dead?") but ask instead, "Who are you, and how many are you?" The answer that comes in Hungarian is indistinct but I can make it out: "We are all here" (a voice adds: "The Holy Spirit knows all languages"). Then I ask, "Is it difficult for you to talk to me like this?" (thinking of the seemingly strenuous breathing that preceded the conversation). A woman answers, quite clearly, and in Hungarian: "We have some difficulties (or obstacles), but how is it for you, do you have obstacles too?" I say, "It was not easy for me to find this way of talking with you, but now I could do it and I am delighted."

Bacci is thinking of the many people who hope to have contact with their lost loved ones and directs attention to the others in the room, not identifying anyone by name, just recalling that they, too, would like to get answers. The voice—the same or a different male voice, it is difficult to say for certain—comes up with a number of names, one after the other. The person named speaks up, often in a voice trembling with hope. "Can I hear Maria (or Giovanni . . .)?" Sometimes a younger voice comes on the air, and a person in the room gives a shout of delight and recognition.

And so it continues for about half an hour. There are breaks taken up by the sound of air rushing as in heavy breathing (Bacci explains, "They are recharging themselves"), but the voices come back. Until it appears that they are really gone.

Bacci moves the dial on the shortwave band, but only static and some shortwave broadcasts come through, as they did during the first hour. He gets up, the lights are switched on; the séance is over.[18]

There is a curious fact relevant to the authenticity of Bacci's anomalous radio transmission. It started, as Bacci's experiments usually did, precisely at 7:30 p.m. But the voices started only one hour later, when our watches showed 8:30 p.m. However, not long beforehand Europe had shifted from winter to summer time. Hence 8:30 p.m. had previously been 7:30 p.m., the exact time the voices manifested themselves. The voices were on time; it was Bacci who attempted communication too soon.

Bacci was subsequently accused of fraud through the manipulation of his radio, as others joined his laboratory in search of financial gain. However, in the last few years Bacci was unable to receive anomalous voices, although he tried his level best. This suggests that his previous experiments may have been genuine. (If fraud was involved from the beginning, the anomalous voices would very likely have continued.) Why the voices ceased is not known, but one may surmise that the reason may have to do with attempts to produce them fraudulently.

INSTRUMENTAL TRANSCOMMUNICATION: WHAT THE EVIDENCE TELLS US

Audio and video transcommunication rely on electronic instruments to establish contact with what appears to be the living consciousness of deceased persons. Reliance on electronic instruments renders the authenticity of the contact open to doubt, much as reliance on mediums does. Electronic instruments are open to willful manipulation, and hence to fraud.

However, in the cases cited here great care has been taken to exclude the possibility of fraud. Engineers have checked the functioning of the instruments and the experimenters repeated the experiments in the presence of witnesses. Some experimenters, such as Hans Otto König, were themselves electronic engineers, and others, including Anabela Cardoso, who was a senior diplomat of her native Portugal, had a reputation to protect and took great care in verifying that the phenomena are authentic.

The impressive number of cases of electronically conveyed communication reviewed in this chapter offers a basis for an initial assessment. We can say that the evidence furnished by credible forms of EVP offers reasonable ground to assume that the consciousness of a deceased person can be contacted and engaged in communication through electronic instruments. Consciousness, it seems, can exist in a form where it gives rise to signals that electronic devices can convert into sound as well as image.

5

PAST-LIFE
RECOLLECTION

The evidence reviewed in the foregoing chapters suggests that it is possible to communicate with a human consciousness even when the body with which that consciousness has been associated is no longer alive. Here we look at an additional strand of evidence in support of this hypothesis: it is furnished by the practice of regression analysis. Hunches of having lived a previous life are reported by many people, but thanks to regression analysis there is now a more systematic and less anecdotal way of gathering and assessing the evidence.

"Regression" in psychotherapy means going back in the mind of a person beyond the range of his or her present lifetime. Normally this calls for shifting the consciousness of the patient into an altered state. Doing so may or may not require hypnosis; often breathing exercises, rapid eye movements, and a well-formulated suggestion are sufficient. When the patient reaches the appropriate state of consciousness, the therapist impels him or her back from memories of the present lifetime to memories that appear to be those of previous lives.

Moving patients back to early childhood, infancy, and even physical birth is seldom a problem for the therapists. Their patients relive the corresponding experiences, even to the extent that, if they stem from early infancy, they exhibit the involuntary muscle reflexes typical of infants.

It appears possible to go back further, to memories of gestation in the womb. And some therapists find that they can take their patients back still further. After an interval of apparent darkness and stillness, strings of anomalous experiences appear, memories that seem to be of other places and other times. The patients not only recount them as if they had read of them in a book or seen them in a film, but they relive the experiences. They *become* the person they experience, even to the inflection of their voice and the language they speak, which may be one they do not know in their present life.

Regression in altered states of consciousness is often taken as evidence that we had previous lives. Having lived before our present life and living again beyond it is an age-old belief. Evidence from the earliest burials shows that our ancestors interred their dead with great care and supplied them with tools and other utilities essential for their next life. Over four-and-a-half thousand years ago, Mesopotamian kings were buried with musical instruments, furniture, and even tools for gambling. Such was the belief in successive lives that soldiers and servants were sometimes ceremonially executed and their bodies placed in the burial chamber so they could serve their masters in their coming life.

On the Indian subcontinent a belief system of creation and emanation is still followed by hundreds of millions. For Hindus death is not the end of existence, but part of a repeating cycle. When life comes to an end, the immortal soul or subtle body of the individual is reborn in a new physical body that can be human or non-human. The cycle of birth and rebirth is *samsara*. This contrasts with the Abrahamic religions (Judaism, Christianity, Islam) where a return to another life on the earthly plane is not recognized.

Psychologists have taken an interest in the phenomena also in the

Western world. Sigmund Freud suggested that irrational fears and phobias might be based on forgotten or sublimated past-life experiences. Through hypnosis Freud was able to take his patients back to the source of these fears and phobias, enabling him to help his patients get rid of them. For Freud's student Carl Gustav Jung, this was evidence of the existence of a collective unconscious in which each individual can access the memories of the broader consciousness that contains all human experiences. But for the mainstream in Western societies, the manifestation of previous life-personalities during hypnotic regression was a form of hysteria or mental illness.

Swedish psychiatrist John Björkhem took a more open-minded approach. Over a long career Björkhem conducted over 600 regressions, many of which involved subjects speaking in languages that were ordinarily unknown to them. A woman named "Mirabella" was able to write in twenty-eight different languages and dialects in her hypnotic trance state.[1]

A SAMPLING OF PAST-LIFE RECOLLECTIONS

Between 1892 and 1910 the French researcher Albert de Rochas used hypnotism to regress a series of individuals. One of them was his cook, Josephine. Josephine proved to be particularly responsive to hypnotic suggestion. In a trance state she described being a man called Jean Claude Bourdon, a soldier in the French Seventh Artillery regiment based in Besançon. She described Bourdon as having been born in Champvent.

Later Josephine was regressed again; this time she recollected being a woman named Philomène Charpigny, who was planning to marry a man by the name of Carteron. In his 1911 book *Successive Lives* de Rochas described how he successfully checked out the details of both regressions and found that both individuals had existed and had experienced the life-events described by Josephine.[2]

De Rochas' most prolific past-lifer was the wife of a soldier, whom he identified simply as "Madame J." Over a series of regressions she described ten previous incarnations. In the first she died at the age of eight months old and was unable to identify who she was. The second session supplied more details. In this she was a girl named Irisee living in Imondo, a small town near Trieste in Italy. She described how she collected flowers for the priests and later offered incense to the gods.

Two other of De Rochas' cases merit mentioning. The first involved a thirty-year-old Frankish warrior chieftain named Carlomee who was captured by Attila the Hun at the Battle of Châlons-sur-Marne in 451 CE. Madame J described how Carlomee had his eyes burned out. The second was that of a French soldier called Michel Berry who was born in 1493. He had a series of love affairs before being killed at the Battle of Marignano in 1515, dying of a lance wound. What is particularly odd about this past life is that Michel stated that he had experienced a precognition that he would die in this way.

De Rochas' most discussed case has been that of eighteen-year-old Marie Mayo. In a trance state she went back to being an eight-year-old girl living in Beirut. She wrote her name in Arabic, but then moved on and became Lina, the daughter of a Brittany fisherman. At the age of twenty Lina married another fisherman called Yvon and a few years later had her first and only child. Sadly, the child died at the age of two. Later she described how her husband was drowned at sea and, in despair, she herself jumped off a cliff into the sea. De Rochas described how Marie became agitated at this point and went into convulsions.[3]

In the middle of the twentieth century a high-profile case of past-life recollections lifted the subject into the mainstream. In 1956 the book *The Search for Bridey Murphy* became a runaway best seller, first in the United States and then across the world. Morey

Bernstein, a businessman from Pueblo, Colorado, described how he had discovered that he had a natural proficiency in hypnotism and that he decided to try out his newfound skills on the twenty-nine-year-old wife of a business associate, "Virginia Tighe." In her hypnotic state Virginia began to speak in a deep Irish brogue. When Bernstein asked who she was, he received the reply that she was a young Irish woman called Bridget (Bridey) Murphy. Bridey said that she was the daughter of Duncan and Kathleen Murphy, Protestants living in the Meadows in Cork. Bridey said that she was born in 1798. Over a series of six taped sessions, Bridey supplied a considerable amount of evidence of her life in early nineteenth-century Ireland. In 1818 she married a Catholic, Brian McCarthy. She offered many details, including the church that Bridey and Michael frequented and the shops where she bought her food and clothing. She described how she traveled with Brian to Belfast, where Brian became a barrister and taught at Queen's University. Bridey died in 1864 after a fall. In the hypnotic state Virginia Tighe, speaking as Bridey, described how she watched her own funeral and looked down at the headstone.[4]

Subsequently the *Chicago Daily News* sent a reporter to Belfast to check on the details supplied by Bridey. Two of the grocery stores mentioned by Bridey were found to have existed at the time of Bridey's death. In one session Bridey had described a two-pence coin that was in use during her lifetime. This again was confirmed by the reporter. Further evidence was discovered in support of Bridey's memories, such as the location of the Meadows just outside Cork. At the time of the regression sessions there was no evidence of such a location. However, researchers then found an 1801 map of the Cork area showing a large area of open pasture called the "Mardike Meadows" to the west of the city. In one session Bridey stated that the Meadows was sparely populated with no nearby neighbors. This was confirmed by the 1801 map.

Such was the interest in the case that Tighe took the name Ruth Simmons in order to protect her identity, but journalists managed to track her down. However, the rival newspaper, *Chicago American,* discovered that Virginia had an Irish aunt, Marie Burns, although in the book she had stated that she had no links to Ireland. Marie, it was claimed, had told her young niece many stories about Ireland. Even more suspicious was that during her childhood Virginia had lived opposite an Irishwoman named Bridey Corkell, whose maiden name had been Murphy.

But things were not quite as clear-cut as the article made them seem. Subsequent research by the *Denver Post* showed that Marie Burns was not of Irish birth, having been born in New York, and that she and Virginia had not met until Virginia ("Bridey") was eighteen.[5]

In 1965 Bernstein published a new edition of *The Search for Bridey Murphy,* and this contained his rebuttal of the criticisms. In this book Bernstein quoted William J. Barker, a journalist who spent many weeks in Ireland checking out every statement Bridey made against authentic documents. Barker wrote that "Bridey was dead right on at least two dozen facts that 'Ruth' (Virginia Tighe, alias Bridey) could not have acquired in this country, even if she had set out deliberately to study up on Irish obscurities."[6]

A researcher who continued to investigate the reality of past-life recollections was Anglo-American psychotherapist Dr. Roger Woolger. In 1989 Woolger published an influential book, *Other Lives, Other Selves.* In this he introduced his model of past-life memories in a therapeutic format.[7] Woolger believed that present-life trauma and psychological problems may have their roots in past lives rather than in the current one. Initially Woolger had been taking a standard Jungian approach, until an event took place that shook his belief system. One of his clients was a woman suffering post-traumatic stress disorder after a major car accident. As part of his therapeutic

approach, Woolger used hypnotherapy. Following his standard pro-
cedure, he hypnotically regressed the woman back to the car crash.
She then relived in detail the events that had led up to the accident.
There was, however, a new element that only emerged during regression. Woolger reported,

> Not only did she relive the accident and release much buried
> trauma held in her body but she also proceeded to re-play the
> experience of watching herself from above as ambulance men
> pulled her body from the wreckage. She then saw her body
> taken to the hospital and undergoing surgery. Next she felt
> herself drifting up to a higher realm and meeting with beings
> of light she recognized as deceased members of her family,
> who told her that her work on earth was not finished and that
> she must return. She remembered the pain of coming back in
> to her body. Prior to the regression she had not "remembered"
> any of this.[8]

This is a classic NDE, coming about in the regressed state of
consciousness induced by hypnosis. Woolger was fascinated by
the implications and used regression analysis on himself. For years
he had been plagued by images of torture and killing. He associated this with his lifelong fear of fire. He then discovered that he had
been a mercenary soldier during the Crusade against the Cathars in
thirteenth-century France.

Most of Woolger's sessions evoked past-life memories that
could not be identified with the lives of then-living persons. The lives
Woolger elicited were often those of, in his words, "African tribesmen,
nomadic hunters, nameless slaves, Middle Eastern traders, anony-
mous medieval peasants . . . lives cut short by famine, plague or
disease at an early age." He also evoked countless lives of young
men dying on the battlefield.[9]

PAST-LIFE RECOLLECTIONS:
WHAT THE EVIDENCE TELLS US

Do memories emerging in altered states of consciousness provide evidence that the individual has lived a previous life? This is a difficult question to decide. Why do only some people have memories of previous lives and not others? If all or at least most people had previous lives we would expect that many among them would have some recollection of them. But only a small segment of people have such "memories." Could it be that most people have forgotten their past lives, as many spiritual traditions maintain? Or that the circumstances under which such memories surface are so specific that they are extremely infrequent? We do know that access to anomalous experiences often calls for entering an altered state of consciousness. For such experiences to be communicated, they need to be vivid enough to be recollected in the waking state. And if they are to be reported without fear of ridicule, they also need to be documented and supported by the experiences of other people. These conditions are not likely to be frequent. Thus it is not prima facie impossible that all or most people have lived previous lives even if only a very few among them can—and wish to—recollect them.

Whether people have had other lives in the past, and whether their recollections are bona fide memories of those lives, is not clear. Yet the evidence is powerful in regard to a basic point. Whether or not the memories that surface in the consciousness of people are memories of their own previous lives, or are fragments from the life of others, memories do surface that are not memories from the present lifetime of the individual. If this is true, then the consciousness of a person who had once lived does not vanish with the death of that person but can be reexperienced by a living person. This conclusion stands whether or not the person whose memories are reexperienced is the same person as the one who reexperiences them.

6

REINCARNATION

As we have seen, there is evidence that at least some, and possibly all, people have previously existed in another body and lived another existence. When anomalous "memories" appear as personal recollections, those who experience them tend to believe that they stem from their own previous life. However, the memories that surface in consciousness are not likely to be past-life recollections. Instead, they appear to be "experiences of the reincarnation-type." The latter are widespread as well. Experiences suggestive of reincarnation are not limited, whether geographically or culturally. They occur in all corners of the planet and among people of all cultures.

There is of course more to reincarnation than memories. For reincarnation to have actually taken place the consciousness of the foreign personality must have entered the body of the experiencing subject. In esoteric literature this is known as the transmigration of the spirit or soul. It is said to occur in the womb, perhaps already at conception or shortly afterward, when the rhythmic pulses begin that develop into the heart of the embryo.

The spirit or soul of an individual does not necessarily migrate to another individual. Buddhist teachings, for example, tell us that the soul or spirit does not always reincarnate on the earthly plane and in a human form. It may not reincarnate at all, evolving to a spiritual domain from where it either does not return or returns only to fulfill a task it was to accomplish in its preceding incarnation.

But what concerns us here is the possibility that reincarnation could truly occur. Can the consciousness that was the consciousness of a living person reappear in the consciousness of another? In his book *The Power Within,* British psychiatrist Alexander Cannon wrote that the evidence on this score is too strong to be dismissed:

> For years the theory of reincarnation was a nightmare to me and I did my best to disprove it and even argued with my trance subjects to the effect that they were talking nonsense. Yet as the years went by one subject after another told me the same story in spite of different and varied conscious beliefs. Now well over a thousand cases have been so investigated and I have to admit that there is such a thing as reincarnation.[1]

VARIATIONS AND VARIABLES IN REINCARNATION-TYPE EXPERIENCES

There are significant differences in the frequency and the quality of experiences of the reincarnation type. Belief appears to be a major factor. Where reincarnation is recognized as a reality, reincarnation-type experiences occur more frequently.

Another variable is the age of the person who comes up with reincarnation-type experiences. Those who do are mostly children between the ages of two and six. After the age of eight the experiences tend to fade and, with few exceptions, vanish entirely in adolescence.

The manner in which the reincarnated personality has died is yet another variable. Those who suffered a violent death seem to be more frequently reincarnated than those who died in a natural way.

Reincarnation-type experiences tend to be clear and distinct in children, whereas in adults they are mostly indistinct, appearing as vague hunches and impressions. The more widespread among them are the *déjà vu*: recognizing a site or a happening one sees for the first time as familiar. The sensation of *déjà connu,* encountering a person for the first time with a sense of having known him or her before, also occurs, but less frequently.

Whether reincarnation-type experiences convey veridical information about places, people, and events has been tested in reference to eyewitness testimonies and birth and residence certificates. The experiences often turn out to be corroborated by witnesses as well as by documents. Sometimes even minute details correspond to real events, persons, and sites.

Vivid reincarnation-type experiences are accompanied by corresponding patterns of behavior. Behaviors suggestive of the reincarnated personality appear even when that personality was of a different generation and a different gender. A young child could manifest the values and behaviors of an elderly person of the opposite sex.

The pioneering research on recent reincarnation-type experiences is the work of Ian Stevenson, a Canadian-American psychiatrist who worked at the University of Virginia School of Medicine. During more than four decades, Stevenson investigated the reincarnation-type experiences of thousands of children, both in the West and in the East. Some of the experiences recounted by the children have been verified as the experience of a person who had lived previously, and whose death matched the impressions reported by the child. Sometimes the child carried a birthmark associated with the death of the person with whom he or she identified, such as an indentation or discoloration on the part of the body where a fatal bullet entered, or a malformation on a hand or the foot the deceased had lost.

In a path-breaking essay published in 1958, "The Evidence for Survival from Claimed Memories of Former Incarnations," Stevenson analyzed the reincarnation-type experiences of children and presented narratives on seven of the cases.[2] These cases turned out to be veridical, with the incidents recounted by the children recorded in often obscure local journals and articles. Stevenson's study was read by Eileen Garrett (the medium whom we have already encountered in regard to medium-conveyed messages). She had heard of similar cases in India and invited Stevenson to come to that country to conduct firsthand research. Stevenson uncovered robust evidence for reincarnation in India as well as in Sri Lanka, Brazil, Ceylon, Alaska, and Lebanon. In 1966 he published his seminal work, *Twenty Cases Suggestive of Reincarnation*.[3] He discovered additional cases subsequently in Turkey, Thailand, Burma, Nigeria, and Alaska and published reports on them in four volumes between the years 1975 and 1983.

A SAMPLING OF
REINCARNATION-TYPE EXPERIENCES

The Case of Ma Tin Aung Myo

A case reported by Stevenson involved a Burmese girl called Ma Tin Aung Myo. She claimed to be the reincarnation of a Japanese soldier killed during the Second World War.[4] The case spans huge cultural differences between the person reporting the experiences and the individual whose experiences she reports.

In 1942 Burma was under Japanese occupation. The Allies regularly bombed the Japanese supply lines, particularly the railways. The village of Na-Thul was no exception, being close to the important railway station at Puang. Regular attacks made life very hard for the villagers, who were trying their best to survive. Indeed, survival meant getting along with the Japanese occupiers. For villager Daw Aye Tin (who was later to be the mother of Ma Tin Aung Myo) this meant discussing the relative merits of Burmese and Japanese food with the stocky, regularly bare-chested Japanese army cook who was stationed in the village.

The war ended, and life returned to a semblance of normality. In early 1953 Daw found herself pregnant with her fourth child. The pregnancy was normal, with the odd exception of a reoccurring dream in which the Japanese cook, with whom she had long lost contact, would follow her and announce that he was coming to stay with her family. On December 26, 1953, Daw gave birth to a daughter and called her Ma Tin Aung Myo. The baby was perfect with one small exception: a thumb-sized birthmark on her groin.

As the child grew up it was noted that she had a great fear of aircraft. Every time one flew overhead she would become agitated and cry. Her father, U Aye Maung, was intrigued by this, as the war had been over many years and aircraft were now simply machines of transport rather than weapons of war. It was therefore strange that Ma was afraid that the aircraft would shoot at her. The child became more and more morose, stating that she wanted to "go home." Later "home" became more specific; she wanted to return to Japan. When asked why this was the case, she stated that she had memories of being a Japanese soldier based in Na-Thul. She knew that she had been killed by machine-gun fire from an aircraft, and this is why she feared airplanes so much.

As Ma Tin Aung Myo grew older she accessed more memories of the life of her previous personality. She was later to tell Ian Stevenson that she remembered that the previous personality came from Northern Japan and that he had five children, the eldest being a boy, and that he had been an army cook. From then on the memories became more precise. She remembered that she (as the Japanese soldier) was near a pile of firewood next to an acacia tree. She described wearing short pants and no shirt. An Allied aircraft spotted him and strafed the area around him. He ran for cover: as he did so, he was hit by a bullet in the groin, which killed him instantly. She described the plane as having two tails. This was later identified as being a Lockheed P-38 Lightning, an aircraft used by the Allies in the Burma campaign.

In her teens Ma Tin Aung Myo showed distinct masculine traits. She cropped her hair short and refused to wear female clothing. This eventually led her to drop out of school.

Between 1972 and 1975 Ma Tin Aung Myo was interviewed three times by Ian Stevenson. She explained that she wanted to be married to a woman and had a steady girlfriend. She said that she did not like the hot climate of Burma nor its spicy food. She much preferred highly sweetened curry dishes. When she was younger she loved to eat semi-raw fish, only losing this preference when a fish bone stuck in her throat.

The actual memories of the Japanese soldier were incomplete in Ma's mind. For example, she had distinct knowledge of his death circumstances but did not remember the soldier's name, the names of his children or wife, or his place of origin in Northern Japan. Stevenson could not inquire into the veracity of these experiences in Japan.[5]

Other Cases in the Indian Subcontinent

Stevenson described how a Sri Lankan girl remembered a life in which she had drowned in a flooded paddy field. She described that a bus had driven past and splashed her with water just before she died. Subsequent research found that a girl in a nearby village had drowned after she had stepped back to avoid a passing bus while walking on a narrow road above flooded paddy fields. She fell backward into deep water and died. The girl who manifested this experience had, from a very early age, shown an irrational fear of buses; she would also get hysterical if taken near deep water. She had a fondness for bread and had a liking for sweet food. This was unusual, in that her family did not like either. However, the previous personality was noted for both of these preferences.[6]

Another typical Stevenson case was that of Swarnlata Mishra, born in a small village in Madhya Pradesh in 1948. When she was three years old she began having spontaneous past-life memories of being a girl called Biya Pathak, who lived in a village more than a hundred miles away. She described that the house Biya lived in had four rooms and was painted white.

She began to sing songs that she claimed she used to know, together with complex dance routines that were unknown to her present family and friends. Six years later she recognized some people who had been her friends in the past life. This stimulated her father to start writing down what she said.

Her case generated interest outside of the village. One investigator who visited the city discovered that a woman who matched the description given by Swarnlata had died nine years previously. Investigations subsequently confirmed that a young girl called Biya had lived in just such a house in that town.

Swarnlata's father decided to take his daughter to the town and to have her introduced to members of Biya's family. As a test the family introduced people who were not related to the child. Swarnlata immediately identified these individuals as being imposters. Indeed some details of her past life were so precise that all were amazed. For example, Swarnlata described a particular wedding that her previous personality had attended in which she had difficulty in finding a latrine. This was confirmed by those in the family who also attended the wedding.

In all, Ian Stevenson recorded forty-nine separate points regarding the life of Biya as described by Swarnlata that were subsequently confirmed by one or more independent witnesses. He considered this as one of his strongest cases related in *Twenty Cases Suggestive of Reincarnation.*[7]

Some Western Cases

Stevenson's investigation of Western cases included one that involved four children of the same family. On May 5, 1957, the sisters Joanna and Jacqueline Pollock were killed by a car on their way to school in Hexham in the North East of England. Joanna was eleven, and Jacqueline was six. The sisters were very close, and the family was devastated by the loss. A year later Florence Pollock discovered that she was pregnant. Her husband, John, was insistent that his wife was carrying twins even though the physicians involved insisted that the pregnancy was normal. John was right; on October 4, 1958, Florence gave birth to twins: Gillian and Jennifer.

Although the girls were identical twins, they had very different birthmarks (identical twins usually have identical birthmarks). Jennifer had two birthmarks, one on her forehead and another on her waist. These were not mirrored on the body of her twin sister, but they mirrored marks on the body of her dead sister, Jacqueline. Jacqueline had a birthmark in exactly the same location as one of them, as well as a scar in the same place as Jennifer's second birthmark.[8]

When the twins were four months old, the family moved from Hexham to Whitley Bay. Two and a half years later the family returned for a visit. Much to the surprise of the parents, the little girls knew their way around the area well. One of the girls pointed and said, "The school is just around the corner." The other pointed to a hill and said, "Our playground is behind there. It has a slide and a swing."

John believed that his two lost daughters had returned. Florence, a practicing Catholic, had great reservations, as the concept of reincarnation was at odds with her beliefs. However, when the twins were four, what happened made Florence accept the possibility of a double rebirth. After the deaths of Jacqueline and Joanna, John had placed their toys in a locked box. It had not been opened since, and the twins had not been aware of its contents. John placed a selection of the toys outside the girls' bedroom and, with his wife watching, called the twins. The girls identified the toys that had belonged to each of them in what appeared to be their previous lives. Jennifer picked up a doll and said, "Oh, that's Mary" and identified another doll as "Suzanne." She then turned to Gillian and said, "And that's your washing machine." Florence thereafter revised her opinion about reincarnation.

Stevenson considered birthmarks one of the most powerful proofs of reincarnation. His interest in birthmarks was followed up by Dr. Jim Tucker, who claimed that a third of all cases from India involve birthmarks that mirrored injuries sustained by the previous personality, and that 18 percent of those among them who had medical records confirm the match.[9]

Tucker, who succeeded Stevenson at the University of Virginia Medical School, focused his investigations on evidence for reincarnation in American children. One case was that of Patrick Christenson, who was born by cesarean section in Michigan in March 1991. His elder brother, Kevin, had died of cancer twelve years earlier at the age of two. Early evidence of Kevin's cancer was presented six months prior to his death when he began to walk and had a noticeable limp. One day he fell and broke his leg. Tests were done, and after a biopsy on a small nodule in his scalp, just above his right ear, it was discovered that little Kevin had metastatic cancer. Soon tumors were found growing in other locations in his body. One such growth caused his eye to protrude and eventually resulted in blindness in that eye. Kevin was given chemotherapy, which resulted in scars on the right-hand side of his neck. He eventually died of his illness, three weeks after his second birthday.

At birth Patrick had a slanting birthmark with the appearance of a small cut on the right side of his neck, exactly the same location as Kevin's chemotherapy scar. He also had a nodule on his scalp just above his right ear and a clouding of his left eye, which was diagnosed as a corneal leukoma. When he began to walk it was with a distinct limp.

When he was almost four and a half he said to his mother that he wanted to go back to his old orange and brown house. This was the exact coloring of the house in which the family had lived in 1979 when

Kevin was alive. He then asked if she remembered him having surgery. She replied that she could not because this had never happened to him. Patrick then pointed to a place just above his right ear. He added that he didn't remember the actual operation because he was asleep.

In 2005 Tucker published a book entitled *Life Before Life: A Scientific Investigation of Children's Memories of Previous Lives*. A case he cited is that of Kendra Carter from Florida. Four-year-old Kendra had started taking swimming lessons at the local pool. She developed an instantaneous attachment to her swimming coach, Ginger. When she was with Ginger, Kendra was happy and contented, but on the days she was not seeing Ginger she was quiet and withdrawn. This behavior worried her parents. One evening she explained to her mother that Ginger had a baby who died and that the coach had been sick and pushed the baby out. This intrigued Kendra's mother. She had been with Kendra at all times during the swimming lessons. It was impossible that Ginger had told Kendra anything about her past; indeed, this was hardly the kind of subject a woman would have told a four-year-old child. However, things became not only strange but somewhat worrisome to Kendra's mother, a conservative Christian, when, in response to the question of how she knew about Ginger's baby, Kendra replied, "I'm the baby that was in her tummy."[10] She then went on to describe how she had been pulled out of Ginger's tummy. It was subsequently discovered that nine years previously Ginger had had an abortion. This was totally unknown to Kendra's mother or any other person around her.

Another case involved an eighteen-month-old boy called Sam Taylor. As his diaper was being changed he looked up at his father and said, "When I was your age I used to change your diapers." Later Sam disclosed details about his grandfather's life that were completely accurate. He said that his grandfather's sister had been murdered and that his grandmother had made milkshakes for his grandfather using a food processor. Sam's parents were adamant that none of these subjects had been discussed in his presence.

When he was four years old, Sam was shown a group of old family pictures spread out on a table. Sam happily identified his grandfather every time with the announcement, "That's me!" In an attempt to test him, his mother selected an old school class photograph showing the grandfather as a young boy. There were sixteen other boys in the photograph. Sam immediately pointed to one of them, once again announcing that that was him. He was right.[11]

REINCARNATION:
WHAT THE EVIDENCE TELLS US

Reincarnation-type experiences can be vivid and convincing to the extent that they appear to be testimony that a previously living personality has been incarnated in the subject. This belief is strengthened by the observation that birthmarks on the body of the subject correspond to the bodily features of the person whom he or she seems to incarnate. This is most strikingly the case when the alien personality suffered bodily injury. The corresponding marks or deformations sometimes reappear in the subject.

Many observers of this phenomenon, including Stevenson himself, held that matching birthmarks are significant evidence for reincarnation. However, the coincidence of birthmarks and other bodily features in a child with the fate of a previously existing person is not necessarily assurance that that person is reincarnated in the child. It could also be that the brain and body of the child with the given birthmarks and bodily features are especially adapted to recall the experience of a personality with analogous birthmarks and deformities. (The nature of this recall—from the deep dimension we shall call the Akasha—is explored in chapter 9.)

This explanation of "experiences of the reincarnation type" is vividly illustrated in an unusual case reported by Stevenson.[12] It concerns a woman who later in life—not in early childhood—appeared suddenly possessed by a consciousness that seems to have been that of a woman who lived 150 years ago.

Uttara Huddar was thirty-two years old when a personality named Sharada appeared in her consciousness. Huddar did not remember a foreign personality before then. She was an educated person with two master's degrees, one in English and the other in public administration, and lectured at Nagpur University in the town where she was born. Sharada, the foreign personality, did not speak the languages Huddar could speak (Huddar spoke Marathi and a little Hindi in addition to English), but she spoke Bengali, a language Huddar spoke only in a rudimentary way. Moreover the Bengali Sharada spoke was not the modern Bengali but that spoken around 1820–1830, the period in which she appears to have lived. She asked for foods and other ethnic particulars of that epoch and did not recognize Huddar's family and friends.

Huddar had a phobia of snakes. Her mother said that while she was pregnant with Huddar she had repeatedly dreamt of being bitten on the foot by a snake. Sharada, the foreign personality, recalled that when she was seven months pregnant she was bitten by a snake while picking flowers. She became unconscious, but had no recollection of having died. She was twenty-two at the time.

This suggests that Sharada was not "incarnated" in Huddar, as before the age of thirty-two Huddar did not know anything of the existence of Sharada, or of the language and the milieu of Sharada. But the shared experience of being bitten by a snake could provide an alternative explanation. As a young woman herself, this experience could have prompted Huddar to "call up" the Sharada personality from the plane we will call the Akasha dimension.

A similar explanation applies to cases where the friends or relatives of the subject and the foreign personality have the same cultural identity. The fact that Virginia Tighe ("Bridey") had Irish acquaintances and relatives is not evidence that she acquired her remarkable knowledge of the Irish milieu by ordinary means. But it is an indication that, thanks to these influences, she was better adapted to recall the experience of an individual who lived in Ireland.

But regardless of the interpretation we attach to the evidence, the fact stands out that, whether the person who is reexperienced has been "reincarnated" in the individual or if the deceased consciousness is just "called up" (assumedly from a deeper level of reality), it is beyond all reasonable doubt that a deceased person can be reexperienced, and seemingly relived, by a living person.

CONSCIOUSNESS BEYOND THE BRAIN
A First Conclusion from the Evidence

What conclusion can we draw from the evidence reviewed in the six chapters of this part? Our conclusion can be summed up as follows: It appears that *in near-death experiences, in the perception of apparitions and visions, in after-death communication, in medium- and instrumentally transmitted communication, in past-life recollections, as well as in reincarnation-type experiences, "something" is experienced, contacted, and communicated with that appears to be a human consciousness. The evidence tells us that this "something" is not a passive record of the experience of a deceased person but a dynamic, intelligent entity that communicates, exchanges information, and may exhibit a desire to communicate.*

If this conclusion is sound, we have good reason to maintain that consciousness persists beyond the brain. How could this be? The persistence of consciousness beyond the brain and body with which it was associated calls for an explanation. In Part 2 we shall suggest an explanation that is not ad hoc and esoteric, but based on insights now emerging at the cutting edge of contemporary science and consciousness research.

PART 2

THE SCIENCE

*Cosmos and
Consciousness*

7

THE REDISCOVERY OF THE DEEP DIMENSION

Our explorations in Part 1 led to the conclusion that on occasion there is "something" that we can experience, contact, and even engage in communication with, and this something appears to be a consciousness no longer associated with a living brain and body. We now ask, what does this mean for our understanding of the world—and of mind and consciousness in the world? What kind of a world is that in which consciousness can persist beyond the death of the body? We turn to the remarkable findings of cutting-edge science to explore a credible answer to this age-old question.

A world in which consciousness can persist beyond a living brain and body is clearly not the world described in the mainstream of modern science. The concept of a world in which material things have a unique location in space and time needs to be reconsidered, along with the concept of mind and consciousness as phenomena produced by a material brain.

The kind of world and the kind of mind and consciousness that can account for our findings can be elucidated in the context of the latest developments in science. New findings are coming to light, in particular in quantum field theory, cosmology, and brain research. A new paradigm is emerging at the leading edge of science—a paradigm where information rather than matter is the basic reality, and where space and time, and the entities that emerge and evolve in space and time, are manifestations of a deeper reality beyond space and time.

THE AKASHA PARADIGM

The paradigm emerging in science is a revolutionary innovation in regard to the mainstream concept of a universe where material entities occupy separate and unique points in space and time, but it is not new in the history of thought. Leading thinkers and scientists have often spoken of the oneness of the world rooted in a hidden or deep dimension. The *rishis* (seers) of India viewed the deep dimension as the fifth and most fundamental element in the cosmos; they called it by the Sanskrit term *Akasha*. We adopt this term, because it can give us a science-based concept of a world where consciousness is part of the basic element—or conceivably *is* the basic element.

THE DEEP DIMENSION IN
HISTORY AND TODAY

The idea of a deep dimension is a perennial insight: the world we observe is not the ultimate reality. It is the manifestation of a reality that lies beyond the plane of our observation.*

Philosophers of the mystical branch in Greek metaphysics—the Idealists and the Eleatic school, including thinkers such as Pythagoras, Plato, Parmenides, and Plotinus—were united in their affirmation of the existence of a deep dimension. For Pythagoras this dimension was the Kosmos, a transphysical, unbroken wholeness, the

---

*See Ervin Laszlo, *Science and the Akashic Field*, Inner Traditions, Rochester, Vt., 2004 and 2007.

prior ground on which matter and mind, and all being in the world, arises. For Plato it was the realm of Ideas and Forms, and for Plotinus "the One." Plato made very clear that the world we experience with our senses is a secondary world, a world we mistake for reality. In the famous dialogue *The Republic,* he offered the metaphor that came to be known as the "parable of the Cave." Plato has Socrates describe a group of people who live chained to the wall of a cave. They watch the shadows projected on the wall by a fire that is behind them, and they come to believe that the shadows are the real world. The real world, however, is behind them; it is a dimension that is hidden from them. The same basic concept is present in the wisdom traditions of the East. In Indian philosophy, for example, the *Lankavatara Sutra* describes the "causal dimension" of the world that gives rise to the "gross" phenomena that meet the eye. Mystics and philosophers in both East and West were certain that the world we observe is illusory, ephemeral, and short-lived, whereas there is a deep dimension that is real, eternal, and eternally unchanging.

At the dawn of the modern age Giordano Bruno brought the concept of a deep dimension into the ambit of modern science. The infinite universe, he said, is filled with an unseen substance called *aether* or *spiritus.* The heavenly bodies are not fixed points on the crystal spheres of Aristotelian and Ptolemaic cosmology, but move without resistance in this unobservable cosmic sphere under their own impetus.

In the nineteenth century Jacques Fresnel revived this idea and called the space-filling unobservable medium *ether.* The ether, in his view, is a quasi-material substance in which the movement of heavenly bodies produces friction. Although the ether is not observable in itself, the friction it produces gives rise to an "ether drag," and the ether drag must produce an observable effect.

Shortly after the turn of the twentieth century, physicists Albert Michelson and Edward Morley tested Fresnel's hypothesis. They reasoned that—given that the earth moves through the ether—the light that reaches it from the sun must display an ether drag: in the direction toward the light source the beams should be reaching us faster than in the opposite direction.

However, the Michelson-Morley experiments failed to detect a drag that could be ascribed to the friction produced by Earth's motion through the ether. Although Michelson noted that this failure does not disprove the existence of the ether, only of a particular mechanistic theory of the ether, the physics community took the negative outcome of the experiment as evidence that the ether does not exist. When Einstein published his special theory of relativity, the concept of the ether was discarded. All movement in space—more exactly, in the four-dimensional spacetime continuum—was said to be relative to a given reference frame. It is not movement against a fixed background such as an ether-filled space.

However, in the second half of the twentieth century physicists revived the idea of an unobservable plane of reality lying beyond the observed phenomena. In the Standard Model of particle physics, for example, the basic entities of the universe are not independent material things even when they are endowed with mass; they are part of the unified matrix that underlies space. The basic entities of the matrix are quantized: they are elementary or composite *quanta* (the smallest identifiable units of matter-energy conventionally called "matter"). The matrix itself is more fundamental than any of the particles that appear in it; the latter are critical points, crystallizations or condensations within it. The matrix, known variously as the *unified* or *grand-unified field,* the *nu-ether,* or the *cosmic plenum,* harbors all the fields and forces, constants, and entities that appear in spacetime. It is not part of physical spacetime; the cosmic matrix is beyond spacetime and prior to it. In the new paradigm we discuss here, the matrix is the cosmic deep dimension: "the Akasha."

THE REDISCOVERY OF THE AKASHA IN CONTEMPORARY SCIENCE

Contemporary physics, especially quantum field theory and quantum-physics-based cosmology, affirms the presence of a fundamental yet intrinsically unobservable plane in the world. The latest theories highlight more and more facets of this plane.

In the fall of 2012 a discovery was made of a new state of matter, known as the FQH (fractional quantum Hall) state. This discovery suggests that the particles that compose "matter" in spacetime are excitations of an underlying non-material matrix. According to the concept advanced by Ying Ran, Michael Hermele, Patrick Lee, and Xioao-Gang Wen of MIT, the entire universe is made up of these excitations in the underlying matrix. The excitations appear as waves as well as particles: technically they are described by Maxwell's equations for electromagnetic waves and by Dirac's equations for electrons.[1]

In the theory put forward by Xioao-Gang Wen of MIT with Michael Levin of Harvard, electrons and other particles are the ends of strings woven into "string-nets." They move in the underlying medium "like noodles in a soup." Different patterns in their behavior account for electrons and for EM waves, as well as for the quarks that make up protons and neutrons and the particles—gluons and W and Z bosons—that make up the fundamental forces. The movement of the string nets corresponds to "matter" and to "force" in the universe. The matrix itself is a string-net liquid in which particles are entangled excitations: "whirlpools." Empty space corresponds to the ground state of this liquid, and excitations above the ground state constitute particles.

In 2013 a new discovery underscored the idea of an Akashic deep dimension in the cosmos. The new discovery—the geometrical object called *amplituhedron*—suggests that spatiotemporal phenomena (the world we observe) are consequences of geometrical relationships in a deeper dimension of the cosmos. Encoded in its volume are the basic measurable features of the universe: the probabilities of the outcome of particle interactions.[2]

The discovery of the amplituhedron permits a great simplification in the calculation of the "scattering amplitudes" in particle interactions. Previously, the number and variety of the particles that result from the collision of two or more particles—the scattering amplitude of that interaction—were calculated by so-called Feynman diagrams, diagrams first proposed by Richard Feynman in 1948. But the number of diagrams required for these calculations is so large that even simple interactions could not be fully calculated. For example, describing the scattering amplitude in the collision of two gluons—which results in four less-energetic gluons—requires 220 Feynman diagrams with thousands of terms. Up to a few years ago this was considered too complex to be carried out even with the help of supercomputers.

In the mid-2000s patterns emerged in particle interactions that indicated a coherent geometrical structure. This structure was initially described by what came to be known as the "BCFW recursion relations" (named for physicists Ruth Britto, Freddy Cacharo, Bo Feng, and Edward Witten). The BCFW diagrams abandon variables such as position and time and substitute for them strange variables—called "twistors"—that are beyond space and time. They suggest that in the non-spacetime domain two fundamental tenets of quantum field physics do not hold: *locality* and *unitarity*. This means that particle interactions are not limited to local positions in space and time, and the probabilities of their outcome do not add up to one. The amplituhedron is an elaboration of the geometry of the BCFW twistor diagrams. Thanks to these diagrams, physicists can now calculate the scattering amplitude of particle interactions in reference to an underlying non-spacetime geometrical object.

A multidimensional amplituhedron in the Akasha could enable

the computation of the interaction of all quanta, and of all systems constituted of quanta, throughout spacetime. The locality and unitarity that appears in spacetime appear as *consequences* of these interactions.

According to Nima Arkani-Hamed of the Institute for Advanced Study and his former student Jaroslav Trnka, the discovery of the amplituhedron suggests that spacetime, if not entirely illusory, is not fundamental: it is the result of geometrical relationships at a deeper level.[3]

THE AKASHA AND
THE MANIFEST WORLD

The concept of an Akashic deep dimension holds vast implications for our understanding of the fundamental nature of reality. The Akasha is not *in* space and time; it is prior to the entities, laws, and constants that appear in spacetime. We can best comprehend this revolutionary concept through its analogy with electronic information systems.

The relation of the unobservable non-spacetime Akasha dimension to the observable spacetime dimension is analogous to the relation of the software of an information system to its behavior. The software determines how the system acts, and these actions are reflected in the display. The computer is active, and the display reflects this activity. But the software does not change as a result of this activity. Until and unless it is modified, it remains what it is: a set of algorithms that governs the behavior of the system. It is the unchanging *logos* and not the changing *dynamics* of the system.

When we apply this analogy to the real world, we conclude that the Akasha is the algorithm that governs the fields and forces that regulate the behavior of particles and systems of particles in the world. It is the logos of the universe, the unchanging software that governs events in spacetime.

THE PHENOMENON
OF ENTANGLEMENT

Cutting-edge science postulates the intrinsic connectedness of all things in spacetime. Interactions among quanta, the smallest identifiable units of matter-energy, turn out to be instantaneous: the quanta are "entangled." This instant interaction transcends the boundaries of the classical concepts of space and time.

Entanglement in space—which is instant interconnection between quanta at any finite distance—has been known since the experimental demonstration of the so-called EPR experiment in the 1970s. A measurement carried out on one of a pair of particles that had previously existed in the same quantum state has an immediate effect on the other particle, regardless of the spatial distance that separates them.

In turn, entanglement in time was confirmed in the spring of 2013 by experiments at the Racah Institute of Physics at the Hebrew University of Jerusalem. Physicists Megidish, Halevy, Sachem, Dvir, Dovrat, and Eisenberg coded a photon in a specific quantum state, and then destroyed that photon. As far as may be ascertained, there was then no photon in spacetime in that particular quantum state. The experimenters then coded another photon for the same quantum state. They found that the state of the second particle was instantly entangled with the state of the first, even though the latter no longer existed. It appears that particles that had never existed in the same quantum state at the same time can still be entangled. The experimenters realized that this could only be if the state of the first photon is conserved in spacetime.[4]

Repeated experiments on entanglement show that not just *some* quanta are entangled beyond the classical confines of space and time, but *all* quanta are. The manifest universe turns out to be an instantly and intrinsically interconnected whole. This is a revolutionary finding.

It calls for a revision of our understanding of the nature and origin of the laws that govern existence and action in the manifest universe. There are new developments at the cutting edge of physics that show that this reassessment is now under way.

HOLOGRAPHIC SPACETIME THEORY

One of the most promising developments is the theory that spacetime is an entangled cosmic matrix. In the emerging concept spacetime is a 3D hologram coded by two-dimensional codes at its boundary. The phenomena we experience are 3D projections of these 2D codes.

Experience with holograms tells us that in a holographic film or medium all the information that creates the observed three-dimensional image is present simultaneously at all points. If spacetime were a holographic medium, that would mean that all quanta, all systems composed of quanta, and all the information that creates quanta and systems of quanta, would exist simultaneously throughout spacetime. Any change in the state of one quanta would be reflected in the state of all quanta. The modification would be instant, since the information that determines the various quantum states is present for all quanta at the same time.

The holographic spacetime hypothesis finds experimental support in the instant modification of the quantum state of distant particles that had initially occupied the same quantum state. This was shown by the physical testing of the so-called EPR (Einstein-Podolski-Rosen) thought experiment. Given that spacetime is a hologram, and that all quanta are entangled with all other quanta, modifications in the state of any quantum will be reflected in the state of all quanta.

The theory that spacetime is a holographic medium was confirmed in the spring of 2013. The German GEO600 gravity wave-detector was built to look for "gravitational waves," ripples in the curvature of spacetime that propagate as waves, traveling outward from the source, as predicted by Einstein in 1916. The GEO600 did find inhomogeneities at the fundamental level in space, but they were not gravity waves. Fermilab physicist Craig Hogan suggested that they might be the ripples that string-theory claims pattern the microstructure of space. This would be the case if the micro-inhomogeneities within spacetimes were 3D projections of 2D codes at the circumference. This hypothesis can be tested against observation.

Let us consider that the volume of spacetime is the distance that light has traveled in all directions from the Big Bang in the approximately 13.8 billion years that have elapsed since then. Suppose further that this circumference is "papered" by 2D codes of Planck-size (where each side of the square is of Planck length: 10^{-35} meter), and that each square codes one bit of information. Events in the volume of spacetime would then be 3D projections of these 2D codes at the circumference. Given that the volume of spacetime is larger than its circumference (the difference can be calculated by dividing the area of the circumference by the volume), it follows that if the 2D codes at the circumference are Planck-dimensional squares, the 3D events within the volume must be of the order of 10^{-16} meter. It turned out that the ripples found by the GEO600 gravity-wave detector are precisely of this size.

Further confirmation of holographic spacetime theory was provided by Yoshifumi Hyakutake and colleagues at Ibaraki University in Japan. They computed the internal energy of a black hole, the position of its event horizon, its entropy, and several other properties based on the predictions of string theory and the effects of virtual particles. Hyakutake, together with Masanori Hanada, Goro Ishiki, and Jun Nishimura, then calculated the internal energy of the corresponding lower-dimensional cosmos with no gravity. They found that the two calculations match, demonstrating that the internal energy of a black hole and the internal energy of the corresponding lower-dimensional cosmos are the same.[5] This provides an indication that black holes, the same as the cosmos as a whole, are holographic.

INTEGRALITY AND WHOLENESS
BEYOND SPACETIME

The holographic hypothesis claims that the entangled three-dimensional events that emerge in spacetime are not ultimate realities, but projections of holographic codes at a deeper level of reality. The codes are not necessarily at the periphery of spacetime (as suggested by Hogan among others), nor are they likely to be in another universe (which was proposed by Brian Greene). They are more cogently considered to be inherent in the fifth element postulated by the rishis: in the Akasha.

The Akasha paradigm views events in spacetime as manifestations of fundamental relations in the Akashic deep-dimension. That dimension is an integral whole, a holographic totality without space and time. The Akashic A-dimension is the unitary *logos* of the cosmos.

8

CONSCIOUSNESS IN THE COSMOS

Your consciousness is not your consciousness.
It is the manifestation of the longing of the cosmos for itself.
*It comes to you through you but not from you.**

The beyond-the-brain consciousness—the consciousness we encountered in our review of near-death experiences, after-death communication, medium-conveyed and instrumental transcommunication, past-life recollections, and in experiences suggestive of reincarnation—is not a material entity in the manifest world. It is an intrinsic element in the Akasha, the deep dimension of the cosmos.

The idea that consciousness belongs to a deeper dimension of reality is a perennial intuition. The great spiritual masters, poets, and even scientists have been telling us that consciousness is not "in" the brain and is not part of the world in which the brain exists. It is part of the mind or intelligence that infuses the cosmos. Consciousness appears

---

*A paraphrase of Khalil Gibran's words about children in *The Prophet:*
  Your children are not your children.
  They are the sons and daughters of Life's longing for itself.
  They come through you but not from you.

123

in space and time as a localized (yet nonlocal) manifestation. Erwin Schrödinger said it clearly: consciousness is one—it does not exist in the plural.

Just as particles and systems of particles in spacetime are projections of codes and relations in the Akashic deep dimension, so the consciousness associated with living organisms is a manifestation—a holographic projection—of the unitary consciousness that does not merely exist in, but actually *is,* that dimension.

THE AKASHIC CONCEPT
OF CONSCIOUSNESS

If consciousness is a holographic manifestation of the unitary consciousness of the cosmos, it is present throughout space and time. Consciousness is present in the mineral kingdom, in the living world, and in the social and ecological systems constituted by human beings and other organisms. It is present at the level of quanta on the one end of the spectrum of size and complexity in nature, and on the level of galaxies on the other end.

But consciousness and the systems and organisms with which it is associated exist on different planes of reality. Particles and the entities composed of particles are part of the manifest world, whereas the consciousness that may be associated with them is an element in the deep dimension.

This insight explains otherwise unresolved puzzles. Among other things, it overcomes the problem of the "hard question" in consciousness research: how something material, such as the brain, can produce something immaterial, such as consciousness. This puzzle does not need to be solved because it rests on false premises. There is no need to account for how the brain produces consciousness because brain and consciousness are on separate planes of reality. The brain does not *produce* consciousness; it *transmits* and *displays* it.

Let us consider this proposition. The standard argument for the claim that the brain produces consciousness is the observation that when the brain is inoperative, consciousness ceases. There are several things wrong with this argument. In the first place, it is not true that consciousness always and necessarily ceases when the brain is not functioning. As we have seen in our review of the NDE, clinical studies show that people whose brain is clinically dead can have conscious experience, and sometimes this experience proves to be a veridical perception of the world.

Second, even if consciousness would cease when the brain is inoperative, this would not prove that consciousness is produced by the brain. When we shut down our computer, cell phone, TV, or radio, the information it displays disappears, yet the information itself does not cease to exist. Just as the information displayed by electronic instruments exists independently of these instruments, so the consciousness displayed by the brain exists independently of the brain that transmits it. Consciousness exists in the cosmos whether or not it is transmitted by a living brain.

EXPERIENTIAL FOUNDATIONS

The claim that consciousness is an intrinsic element of the cosmic deep dimension has foundations in our own experience. We access consciousness in a fundamentally different way from the way we access things in the world. To begin with, consciousness is private: only "I" can experience it.

But unlike other things, I do not observe my consciousness, I *experience* it. The difference is not negligible. Observation is a third-person act: the observer is separate from the person, thing, or event that he or she observes. The brain, unlike the consciousness that is associated with it, can be observed in this mode. In observing the brain we see gray matter made up of myriad networks of neurons and subneuronal assemblies.

But we do not and cannot observe the consciousness associated with them.

There is further support for the claim that consciousness is not part of the manifest spacetime world. It is the evidence—presented and discussed in Part 1—that consciousness exists not only in association with the brain but can persist beyond it. If consciousness were produced by the brain it would cease when the brain ceased to function. We have seen, however, that in some notable cases consciousness continues to exist beyond a functioning brain. This is not an anomaly. Consciousness is not part of the brain and is not produced by the brain. It is merely transmitted and displayed by the brain, and it exists whether or not it is transmitted and displayed by the brain.

THE PRINCIPAL PROPOSITIONS OF THE AKASHIC CONCEPT OF CONSCIOUSNESS

Consciousness Is Transmitted and Displayed by the Brain

If consciousness is not in, and is not a part of, the manifest world, then consciousness is either in a transcendent spiritual realm described in the Abrahamic religions or is part of a non-manifest dimension of the cosmos. The Akashic concept is that consciousness is part of the cosmos, even a fundamental part. But it is not the observable spacetime part.

In contemplating this proposition let us return to the analogy of information transmitted by a radio or another instrument. We know that a radio *reproduces* the sounds of the symphony rather than *producing* that symphony. The symphony exists independently of its reproduction and continues to exist when the radio is turned off. Of course, when the radio is turned off we no longer hear the sounds of the symphony. But this does not mean that the symphony would cease to exist.

The Deep Dimension Is a Cosmic Consciousness

As suggested above, the deep dimension of the cosmos is a consciousness. It receives information from the manifest dimension, and it "in-forms" the manifest dimension. In the perspective of the manifest world the deep dimension is an information field or medium; it "in-forms" things in the world. But "in itself," this dimension is more than a network of in-forming signals. It is a consciousness in its own right.

This tenet is supported by the experience of our own consciousness. We noted that we do not *observe* our consciousness—we *experience* it. We also do not *observe* the Akasha (it is a "hidden" dimension), but we *experience* it: more precisely, we experience its effect on things we *can* experience: things in the manifest dimension. Let us suppose, then, that we could experience not only the manifest spacetime world but also the deep dimension itself. That would presuppose that we are a divine or supernatural being, co-extensive with the cosmos. If we *were* the cosmos, we could introspect on its deep dimension. Our introspection would very likely reveal what introspection reveals in regard to our own experience: not sets and flows of signals, but the qualitative flow we know as our consciousness. Our cosmic-level introspection would reveal a cosmic consciousness.

Cosmic Consciousness In-forms the Manifest World

Just how does consciousness in the deep dimension in-form things in the manifest world? This is a difficult question, as it concerns the physical effect of a non-physical agency. It is elucidated, however, by recent explorations at the frontier where quantum physics encounters neuroscience. The basic concept is the work of physicist Roger Penrose and neuroscientist Stuart Hameroff. They claim that their theory explains how a basically immaterial consciousness can enter into and in-form the material (or quasi-material) world.[1]

The relevant concept is Penrose's "Orchestrated Objective Reduction" (Orch OR). This concept extends Einstein's general relativity to the Planck scale, the basic level of spacetime. According to Penrose, a particle in one state or location is a specific curvature in spacetime geometry, and the same particle in another location is a curvature in the opposite direction. The superposition of the curvatures in both locations make for simultaneous curvatures in opposite directions, and these constitute bubbles or blisters in the fabric of spacetime.[2] These bubbles or blisters are the quanta that populate the physical world. They are entangled and nonlocal, but they are unstable: they collapse on interaction into the fine-structure spacetime, assuming one particular state at one particular place and time.

Penrose suggests that each quantum collapse introduces an element of consciousness into spacetime. If this is the case, we would have a physics-based explanation of how consciousness in the deep dimension enters the manifest world. We have said that every quantum, every atom, and every multiatomic structure, including our own brain and body, are "in-formed" by the deep dimension. This "in-formation" occurs due to the sensitivity of the subneuronal structures of our brain to quantum-level fluctuations. They are responsive to the orchestrated objective reduction through which consciousness enters the manifest world at the level of the fine structure of spacetime.

Theories accounting for the presence of consciousness in the world will no doubt be further developed in coming years. But it is not likely that their further development would change the basic insight: that consciousness is not produced by the brain. Consciousness is a cosmic phenomenon merely transmitted and elaborated by the brain.

Consciousness is a cosmic dimension, and the brain is a local entity. The consciousness associated with the brain is a localized manifestation of the Akasha, the deep dimension of the cosmos.

PART 3

THE
EXPLANATION

9

REEXPERIENCING CONSCIOUSNESS

The Recall from the Akasha

The objective of Part III of this study is to explore the science outlined in Part II for its ability to shed light on the beyond-the-brain phenomena reviewed in Part I. In light of the Akasha paradigm, we can consider contact and communication with a consciousness not associated with a living brain a bona fide phenomenon in the world.

Human consciousness, we have said, is a localized manifestation of the integral consciousness we call the Akasha. The manifestations of consciousness we have encountered in medium- and instrument-conveyed experiences, in past-life recollections, and in reincarnation-type experiences are localized instances of this cosmic consciousness.

Because our individual consciousness is an integral part of the holographically entangled Akasha, everything that takes place in our consciousness is integrated with other instances of localized consciousness in the universe.

This proposition may appear mind-boggling, but it is within the scope of actual experience. It is familiar in the sense that it can be compared to artificial information systems. Consider a battery-operated laptop computer, a tablet, or smartphone. If the device runs on its batteries it will run down: its batteries will be exhausted. The batteries of the electronic device are analogous to the life energy of a living organism. Both can be recharged for a while, but not indefinitely. Sooner or later the energy feeding the system will be exhausted, and then the electronic system will become inert, and the organism will die. When the organism approaches its end state, its consciousness fades and flickers, much as the display of the electronic device when its batteries are nearly down. When the organism has fully exhausted the energies available to it, its consciousness vanishes. The organism is dead, and the electronic device is said to be "dead" as well. The systems no longer process information.

Death for the organism and the corresponding "dead" state for an electronic instrument is the classical interpretation of what happens when the energy store in a system is exhausted. In regard to the electronic device, we know that the consequences are not necessarily what they appear to be. Everything that has been programmed into the device could have been saved—for example, by uploading it into an application such as Dropbox, iCloud, or another cloud-computing program. Then the algorithms and programs that make up the intelligence of the device persist even when the system is down and can be recovered when the device is recharged. They can be recovered not only by the devices that entered the information but by any device with an active power source.

A similar process of information conservation applies to nature. Although an organism cannot be revived once it has entered the terminal state, its memory stores could have been saved into the Akasha, and they could be "called up"—reexperienced—by any organism with an active brain and nervous system. Everything in the flow of sensations, feelings, and information that constitutes a human consciousness is "saved into" that deep dimension. This is not a separate add-on process but an intrinsic and continuous one. Human consciousness is not the product of the human brain, but an intrinsic element of the consciousness that pervades the cosmos.

This explains our experiencing elements of consciousness that are not elements of *our* consciousness. We know that in a cloud-computing information system all files are linked with all other files, and all can be recalled. All that is needed is the code—the "username" or "password"—for the given file to appear. We know this when we "call up" sites and information from the Internet. The Internet itself is not present to our senses; it is an invisible net that encompasses, saves, and can display all the files that have been uploaded into it.

This is an analogy for the process that takes place in regard to the information processed by the brain. The cerebral networks process and store the information received by the organism, and some and potentially all of this information can be retrieved. When we think of a person, a site, or an event, we envision that person, site, or event together with the related persons, sites, and events. We retrieve them from our memory stores. In altered states of consciousness we expand our memory stores. We can also recall persons, sites, and events that were not part of our own lifetime experience.

The consciousness associated with our brain is an intrinsic element in a holographically entangled cosmic information field. It is linked to the "rest of the world." This means that in principle we can call up anyone's consciousness—any "file" that has been "saved" into the cosmic information field—regardless of whether the person who has entered the information is alive. This reexperiencing is not just abstract possibility: the potential for it is demonstrated in the work of transpersonal psychologists and psychiatrists. When they shift their patients into altered states of consciousness they expand their consciousness to an extent that, in the words of Stanislav Grof, it seems to encompass the whole universe.

Contact and communication with the localized forms of the cosmic consciousness is facilitated by entering an altered state of consciousness of one's own. Communication is prompted by love, grief, and other strong emotions. Mediums seem able to achieve communication at will. Communication can also be achieved through electronic instruments, where an instrument manifests the information called up by the experimenter. And experiencers of reincarnation testify that communication can also be brought about by the coincidence of one's bodily features with the features of a deceased person, especially if that person lived in one's environment and met with a violent death.

The notion of "calling up" is apt. Through our consciousness we are calling up elements of consciousness that may be elements of our own consciousness (in which case they are our own long-term memories) or elements of other people's consciousness. All elements of consciousness are conserved in the deep dimension and are integrated with all other elements. They can all be called up—reexperienced—by everyone. This recall is not limited either in space or in time. Our localized consciousness is an integral part of the consciousness that in-forms the universe.

10
DEATH AND BEYOND
The Return to the Akasha

Following our review of the recall elements of consciousness from the Akasha, we now look at the inverse process: how we are returning elements of our own consciousness into this Akashic dimension. As remarked, every thought, feeling, and intuition that appears in our mind is spontaneously transferred into the Akasha. In this context the term transfer is misleading. Everything in our consciousness is intrinsically linked with—is an intrinsic part of—the Akashic deep dimension. Thus nothing needs to be transferred; everything is already there, saved instantly and spontaneously.

When an individual dies, this process of instant sharing comes to an end. At that point the totality of the information that has been saved into the deep dimension returns to that dimension. Here again, the term "return" is misleading, since there is not a question of a bundle of information "returning" from one place to another. The totality of the information that made up our consciousness is conserved in the Akasha and is integrated with the consciousness of all other humans and other beings in spacetime. With the death of the body the connection between our individual consciousness and the cosmic consciousness remains unbroken; only our body and brain are shifted out of it. Dying is not the end of existence; it is a return of the consciousness localized in the individual to the cosmos.

The human body has a finite span of existence, whereas the cosmic consciousness may be infinite. Thus there is not only a point in time when consciousness in the deep dimension enters into and begins to "in-form" the body, but also a point when that process of "in-formation" comes to an end. After that terminal point, the quanta, the atoms, the molecules, and the cells that make up the body continue on their own paths. They are separately in-formed by the Akasha and conserve the consciousness that corresponds to their own state. The consciousness that had in-formed the whole body does not vanish: it then follows its own trajectory. It remains an intrinsic part of the consciousness of the cosmos.

HALLMARKS OF THE REENTRY INTO THE AKASHA

There are firsthand reports on the basic features of the return of an individual's localized consciousness to the Akasha. These are reports by people who have almost died but came back: reports on their NDE. There are also indirect reports—"transcommunications"—from people who did die. These come from mediums, from people in altered states of consciousness, and from children—all who could recall some elements of their own death: the return of their consciousness to the Akasha.

As we noted in chapter 1, NDEs, though diverse, have common elements: Raymond Moody called them "traits." The principal traits are a sense of being dead, peace and painlessness, the out-of-body experience, the tunnel experience, encountering people of light, rising rapidly into the heavens, a reluctance to return, and the panoramic life review. Further traits of the experience include joyous encounters with family members and other loved ones, and also frustrating encounters with people who do not notice the attempts of the deceased to come in contact with them—they fail to perceive his or her discarnate presence. But it is the feeling of deep peace and tranquility in many if not all NDEs that usually prevails. It makes most of those who experience them reluctant to return.

There are physiological correlates that explain some of the above traits, among them the tunnel experience and the experience of radiant light. As already remarked, a surge of activity has been found in the brain of dying persons with increased blood flow. This could account for experiencing the tunnel and the radiant light at its end. But increased blood flow does not account for the other traits of the NDE. There is no physical or physiological explanation for the out-of-body experience, for contact and communication with deceased individuals, for communication with beings of light, and for the panoramic life review. Yet these features suggest that the consciousness that was associated with a living brain and body continues to be present. And it is present more intensely and effectively than during the lifetime of the individual.

THE CASE OF "E.K."

A joyous expansion of being is frequently felt in after-death experiences. The following report channeled by Jane Sherwood illustrates this point.

> I found myself awake in the transition state . . . I thought myself still weak and ill, but I arose from my rest feeling marvelously refreshed and happy and I wandered for awhile in the something-nothing surroundings of this queer world and was unable to make any sense of it. The brooding silence drugged me into unconsciousness for a long time, because when next I woke my body felt quite different, no longer frail and weak as I had supposed, but vigorous and ready for anything as though I had suddenly stepped back into youth.

E.K. then found himself on a hillside and described the view:

This was no earthly beauty. There was light *on* things and *in* them so that everything proclaimed itself vividly alive. Grass, trees, and flowers were so lighted inwardly by their own beauty that the soul breathed in the miracle of perfection . . .

I am almost at a loss to describe the heavens as I saw them from my hillside. The light radiated from no one direction, it was a glowing, universal fact, bathing everything in its soft radiance so that the sharp shadows and dark edges which define objects on earth were missing. Each thing glowed or sparkled with its own light and was lighted as well by the circumambient splendor. The sky, as I looked upward, was like a pearl gleaming with opalescent colors. There was a suggestion of unfathomable depth of space as the shimmering colors parted their transparencies to show the infinite abyss.[1]

These experiences suggest that the individual has left behind the manifest world of local and material things and entered a realm where things do not have matterlike consistency and do not exist at unique points in space and in time.

TWO PATHS

The joyous quality of near-death and after-death experiences is striking, but it does not hallmark the experience of all people. Human consciousness, it seems, can take more than one path when it leaves the body. While some experiences are fulfilling and joyous, others manifest discomfort and suffering.

For thousands of years the religious and spiritual traditions of the world have been telling us that the soul's journey beyond the body can lead up to a heavenly realm, or it can lead down to a valley of woe and suffering. Is there a discernabile reason for entering on the one or the other of these paths?

Tibetan Buddhism describes the transition beyond earthly life as passage through the bardo. *Bardo* means "intermediate," or "transitional," or "in-between" state. It is the state of existence between two earthly lives. After death and before its rebirth, consciousness is not associated with a physical body and experiences a variety of things in its discarnate state. It may experience clear perceptions of the immediate surroundings, as well as disturbing hallucinations. The latter may precede rebirth that comes in an undesirable form and in unfavorable circumstances.

In Tibetan Buddhism the entity that transits from one life to another is the *gandharva*. Its existence is a logical assumption, since there cannot be any discontinuity between the death of one individual and his or her rebirth. The intervening period is the period of transition or transmigration: the period of the sixth bardo. It is preceded by five other periods that extend throughout the preceding lifetime of the individual. These are: the *shinay bardo*, the bardo of birth and life; the *milam bardo*, the bardo of the dream state; the *samten bardo*, the bardo of meditation; the *chikkhai bardo*, the bardo of the moment of death; the *chonyid bardo*, the bardo of luminosity hallmarked by visions; and finally the *sidpa bardo*, the bardo of transmigration.[2]

In the spiritual tradition of the West we get a different account of the journey of the soul, spirit, or consciousness beyond death. The classical account comes from Hellenic mythology. It speaks of Hades, the domain of the dead, traversed by five great rivers: the Styx, the Acheron, the Cocytus, the Phlegethon and the Lethe. (Contrary to popular belief, it was not in the Styx that the ferryman who conveyed the dead to the other side plied his trade but in the lesser-known Acheron.) Sojourn in Hades was not for eternity. Within its vast timelessness there was a period when, once completed, the deceased (whom the Greeks called "the shade") would be expected to go back and re-live its life. However, before returning, the shade had to drink from the waters of one of the five rivers: the Lethe, the river of oblivion. The waters were to wash away all memories of the shade's past life, and allow it to be reborn into the same life path. The Roman poet Virgil described the scene:

> Now did Aeneas descry deep in a valley retiring, a wood, a secluded copse whose branches soughed in the wind, and the Lethe River drifting past the tranquil places. Hereabouts were flitting a multi-tude [of phantoms] without number . . . Aeneas moved by the sud-den sight, asked in his ignorance what it might mean, what was that river over there and all that crowd of people swarming along its banks. Then [the ghost of] his father, Ankhises said: "They are the souls who are destined for Reincarnation; and now at Lethe's stream they are drinking the waters that quench man's troubles, the deep draught of oblivion . . . They come in crowds to the river Lethe, so that you see, with memory washed out they may revisit the earth above."[3]

When the waters of the Lethe wash away all memories of the shade's just concluded life, he or she is reborn in a new body and begins a new life, oblivious of having lived before.

THE PATH OF REBIRTH

The belief that the soul, spirit, or consciousness is reborn in another body is not limited to spiritual doctrines: it is a widespread, nearly uni-versal belief. It occurs in nearly all corners of the planet and among people of nearly every culture. In Ancient Greece it was a central belief of the Orphic religion, and in the Jewish Kabbalah it was known as

Gilgul. On the extreme western fringes of Europe, the Celts, as part of their Druidic theology, believed that the human soul always passes from one body to another, and farther north the Norsemen shared the same belief. In modern times belief in the transmigration of souls remains present among the Yoruba of West Africa, the shamanic traditions of the Native Americans of Alaska and British Columbia, the Druse in Lebanon, and the Alevis in Turkey.

Religious and spiritual beliefs in what is said to be the transmigration of the soul are supported by secular evidence. It is furnished by a special variety of the reincarnation-type experience. In the standard variety there is little or no information about what happens to consciousness between lives; consciousness simply reappears in another body, typically in that of a child. The journey that has led from the previous and now deceased body to the new body is seldom revealed. Yet if this journey takes up a finite amount of time there should be some traces of it in the transiting consciousness. Apparently, there are, although they are seldom reported. Thousands of cases of reincarnation have been reported by hundreds of expert investigators, and some among them describe the interval between the demise of the former personality and his or her reappearance in another. The most frequent interval appears to be under a year, but periods of several years have been reported as well. And in the case of historical personages the interval may extend to centuries.

Some children report "intermission memories" that offer glimpses of the experience between death and rebirth. The majority of the reports come from children in some parts of Asia. Jim Tucker and Poonam Sharma collected an impressive number of what they call "reincarnation-type experiences with memories from the intermission between lives."[4]

Of the over 2,500 experiences of the reincarnation type collected by Tucker and Sharma, twenty-six include recollections of the interval between the death of the previous personality and his or her reappearance in a child. Intermission-type memories are typically of four kinds: memories of the deceased person's funeral, followed by experiences of other earthly events, then memories of existence in an extraterrestrial realm, and finally memories of conception or rebirth. Reincarnation-type experiences with memories of intermission are generally clearer and more veridical than reincarnation-type experiences without intermission memories. The children who recall them know the previous personality by name and even by nickname and give a clear and verifiable account of the previous personality's mode of death. Tucker and Sharma found that 74 percent of the accounts of the death of the previous personality were accurate in most details, and 10 percent were accurate in every detail.

Intermission-type experiences are clearer also in regard to birthmarks or birth defects that correspond to wounds suffered by the previous personality. Children with intermission-type memories exhibit more behaviors relating to the life of the previous personality and show fewer differences between the previous personality and their own family.

The difference between reincarnation-type experiences with intermission memories and those without such memories regards mainly the clarity and strength of the experiences. There are no significant differences in the ages of the children who remember the experiences and in the number of birthmarks or birth defects on their bodies. There are few differences concerning the distance between the place where the previous personality had lived and where the child now lives: the average distance proved to be 201 kilometers in experiences of the intermission kind and 255 kilometers in experiences without intermission memories.

NEAR-DEATH EXPERIENCES AND EXPERIENCES OF THE REINCARNATION TYPE

Reincarnation-type experiences are sufficiently similar to near-death experiences to warrant viewing them as experiences of the same kind.

However, there are some notable differences. NDEs often have a component of return or recall to existence in the physical body, and this is missing in reincarnation-type experiences. Other differences regard the quality of the experiences. We have seen that in many near-death experiences the quality of the experience is positive, and sometimes it is extraordinarily joyous. This is not so in reincarnation-type experiences. Thirty-five reincarnation-with-intermission-type experiences analyzed by Tucker and Sharma had what the children described as "a subjective sense of being dead," but only two of the thirty-five had a positive quality such as a feeling of peace and painlessness. Also missing in the reincarnation-type experiences is the sense of being enveloped in light, seeing beautiful colors, and entering into the light. They seldom suggest a feeling of harmony and unity with the cosmos. Rather, the intermission between lives appears to be a period of discomfort and suffering.

What reason can we find for these divergences between NDEs and reincarnation-type experiences? The answer has been traditionally given in spiritual and religious doctrines. In the Eastern traditions the key concept in this regard is karma. The quality of the subject's karma, decided on the basis of the spiritual and moral quality of his or her life, seems to decide under what circumstances he or she returns.

The quality of one's karma may also decide whether one returns altogether. Return to earthly existence may be a consequence of an insufficiently accomplished life, calling for another cycle of existence to rectify. Rebirth may be a second chance—and then a third and perhaps a tenth chance—on the journey of the subject's consciousness toward the higher realms, which Buddhists call nirvana and we now recognize as the deep dimension of the cosmos.

The path of no return is highly valued by spiritual masters. The Tibetan Tulku Thondup advised, "if you are a highly accomplished meditator—one who has refined and perfected the enlightened nature of the mind—you must remain in that enlightened state without wavering. If you do, instead if rebirth, you could attain buddhahood."[5]

This is essentially the message conveyed also by Western mediums channeling discarnate entities. According to the entity called Seth, channeled by Jane Roberts, the state of being human is but one stage in the process of progressive soul or spirit development. When this stage is finished, there is a passage to another plane of existence with more exalted opportunities for development.[6]

The paths of the journey of consciousness beyond the body appear to diverge, but ultimately they may converge. Even if there is a cyclic return to earthly existence through reincarnation, for periods of testing and perfecting, when that cycle is complete human consciousness returns to where it came from: to the Akasha, the deep dimension and integral consciousness of the cosmos.

∞

We began this inquiry by asking the Big Question: Does our consciousness—mind, soul, or spirit—end with the death of our body? Or does it continue in some way, perhaps in another realm or dimension of the universe? We can now say that the answer to the Big Question is positive. Our consciousness does not end with the demise of our body; it continues to exist in another dimension of the cosmos: in the deep dimension we call the Akasha. Although there is no absolute certainty about any question regarding the nature of reality, and especially the nature of this deeper reality, the certainty we have in regard to the Big Question is solid enough to give us assurance that the answer we have found is likely to be right.

CONSCIOUS IMMORTALITY

The Dawn of a New Era

Although the Big Question has not been finally and definitively answered, nor will it ever be, we have good reason to believe that we are immortal. In the final count, who we are is not defined by our body but by our mind. And whereas our body is mortal, our mind, like all consciousness in the cosmos, persists indefinitely and perhaps infinitely beyond space and time.

What does it mean to have a consciousness that persists beyond the body? This is a kind of immortality, but what does it mean for us as individuals, and as a species? Surely, an awareness of our immortality changes our concept of who we are, and what the world is. This is a major change, a veritable transformation, since the still dominant materialist view does not allow for the existence of an immortal mind. But if that view were correct, consciousness could not persist beyond the body, and evidence that it does would be an enigma. But the evidence is robust, and the dominant view is likely to be mistaken. Our consciousness does not disappear when we die. This is an age-old insight, and if we would recall and revive it, a new era would dawn for us as individuals, and for the human species as a whole.

THE NEED FOR A NEW ERA

It has been said that the only constancy in this world is the constancy of change. Change is constant, but its pace varies greatly. There are epochs of relative stability and epochs of sudden and revolutionary change. This holds for the evolution of galaxies the same as for the evolution of living species. It also holds for the evolution of human societies.

We live in an era of accelerating change. New societies, shaped by new ways of thinking, acting, and valuing, spring up overnight. But this development is largely lacking conscious purpose. There is no consensus as to where it will lead, nor to where it should lead. This is a dangerous lacuna. In the past there was a more definite vision of where we should be going. This vision was inspired by values proclaimed in spirituality and religion, and as of the nineteenth century also it was informed by secular ideals. The ideals were sometimes exploited by power-hungry elites, and the aftermath prompted the question: Is it better to drift rudderless on the seas of change, or steer toward an end that may be mistaken and possibly damaging? Ideally, we should steer by a star that serves the best interests of all. That, however, is not easy to come by.

At a time of sudden and unforeseen change, there is a role for positive thinking. Positive futures need to be envisaged, and subjected to scrutiny and testing. Today, if people are asked what we need to achieve a better future, most of them would reply that we need cheaper and more abundant energy, more wealth, better technology, and more efficient information to drive action. We have tried applying these answers to the problems we face, and on the whole they have failed. The world continues on a downward course toward conflict, crisis, and degradation.

It is time to adopt a better vision for our individual and collective destiny—a vision that does not dictate preconceived courses of action but bolsters the human spirit and gives it confidence in the value of life and the purpose of existence. Such a vision could derive from the recognition that we have an immortal mind and consciousness.

In the past, belief in immortality was just that: a belief. But what if immortality had a foundation in fact? What if it had the kind of credibility that science can offer? This, we have seen, is a real possibility. Would it not inspire and promote positive values and responsible behaviors?

A SHORT HISTORY OF FOUR ERAS

At the dawn of history we existed as immortal beings, but we did not know it. Later our existence was grounded in the intuitive belief that we are immortal. And then came the great disillusionment brought by modern-age rationality: we began to exist as consciously mortal beings. The era of conscious mortality is still here today. But must it be here tomorrow?

The Era of Unconscious Immortality
In the roughly five million years since our forebears diverged from the higher apes, we were not conscious of either our mortality or our immortality. We just existed, without consciously thinking about the nature of our existence. We did have an immortal mind, but we were not conscious of it. Yet knowing that our mind is immortal would not have surprised us, for we did not have a sense of duality: we did not divide the world into "me" and "not me." We did not feel ourselves separate from the world. We existed embedded in nature, feeling ourselves intrinsic elements in a sphere of seamlessly whole existence. We lived our oneness with the world without recognizing that oneness.

The era of unconscious immortality lasted millions of years, from the early Stone Age to the Neolithic, and in some parts of the world well beyond that. Then another era dawned.

The Era of Intuitive Immortality

Some thirty to fifty thousand years ago we became aware that a time comes when our spirit leaves our body. But we did not think of death as the end of existence. We believed in the persistence of spirit beyond the body. We buried our dead but did not take leave of them. We sent them on their journey endowed with the spiritual as well as the material resources they needed to continue their existence.

Our elders handed down their intuitive beliefs in the legends and stories of life beyond death. In time some of these legends became doctrines that had the stamp of spiritual authority. Some of the doctrines hardened into dogmas and were accepted as prescriptions for the way to think and to act. The doctrines separated the believers from the nonbelievers and from the differently-believers and produced endless strife and conflict. Yet there were no significantly nonbelieving doctrines; the conflict concerned only what we believed. In one way or another all our doctrines affirmed belief in the immortality of the human soul or spirit.

The Era of Conscious Mortality

The era of intuitive immortality lasted hundreds of thousands of years. It was transcended and began to decline when, two and a half thousand years ago, a reason- rather than faith-based system of thought emerged on the shores of the Mediterranean. Initially as Greeks and later also as Romans, we explored the interpretation of the nature of our experience in rational terms. In the Middle Ages our thinking was colored by Christian doctrines, but rather than surrendering its rational bent, we applied it to the Christian teachings.

At the dawn of the modern age we adopted a belief system based on observation and later on experiment and measurement rather than belief. We developed what we considered the scientific view of the world.

Modern science held that, of all the things that enter into our experience, only those are real that we can see, hear, touch, and taste. This belief vastly reduced the range of our experience. Many elements and aspects of human experience were ignored, suppressed, or discarded. They did not fit into the scientific view of the world, according to which the real world consists only of matter, and of things constituted of matter. Soul, spirit, mind, and consciousness are illusion. The body alone is part of the real world, and the body is mortal. Thus we, as all living organisms, are irreversibly and irrevocably mortal: when our body dies, we die. This was the era of conscious morality, and in many parts of the world it lasts to this day.

But the era of conscious morality is now drawing to an end. It is transcended by new insights that lend scientific credibility to the idea of an immortal mind. If this idea were to be recognized by a critical mass of people, a new era would dawn for humankind.

The Era of Conscious Immortality

The era of conscious immortality would mark a new phase in the history of human life on this planet. In this era we would transcend the still dominant belief system of mainstream modern science and realize that consciousness is a basic and enduring element in the cosmos, and that our own consciousness is an intrinsic part of it.

The era of conscious immortality would change our relations to each other and to nature. We would not become saints and angels, but we would evolve into beings who know that they possess an immortal mind. We would no longer live in fear of death, in the fear that our days are numbered and lead to nothingness. We would not be prey to the desperate desire to grab all we can while we can, since "we only live once."

We would lead a more responsible life, caring for the well-being of other people and for our life-supporting environment. We would know that when our body dies, we do not leave this world but only transit into another phase of our existence. Realizing that our consciousness is immortal would give us the assurance we need to experience joy in living and tranquility in dying. It would give us the enduring satisfaction of being able to contribute to a world we can experience and enjoy over and over again, in this life and in lives to come.

Confirming Views from Extraordinary Sources

The views reported in this appendix come from extraordinary sources. They are of interest because they address key questions of our existence on the basis of information that appears to be accessible to the entities that report on them but are not accessible to most other people. These questions include:

- the persistence of consciousness after death
- the separate destiny of body and of consciousness
- the dubious reality of the material world
- the nature of energy and thought
- the possibility of communication beyond space and time

A VIEW FROM THE SOURCE "BERTRAND RUSSELL"

The philosopher Bertrand Russell was known for his extraordinary intelligence in his long life. It was not known, however, that his intelligence was extraordinary to the extent that it would survive the death of his body.

The view cited here was expressed by Russell in the early 1970s. He was dead at the time, having passed away in February of 1970. This excerpt was channeled by Rosemary Brown, a well-known medium. Russell was aware that the authenticity of his message would be challenged as conceivably fraudulent and used his intellectual acumen to dispel this suspicion.

> You may not believe that it is I, Bertrand Arthur William Russell, who am saying these things, and perhaps there is no conclusive proof that I can offer through this somewhat restricted medium. Those with an ear to hear may catch the echo of my voice in my phrases, the tenor of my tongue in my tautology; those who do not wish to hear will no doubt conjure up a whole table of tricks to disprove my retrospective rhetoric.[1]

A determined agnostic, Russell was skeptical about the probability (if not, as he said, of the possibility) of life after death. He said that he was positive that he knew the answers to many questions, including the vexing one concerning the probability of taking up a new life after this one has ceased. Yet he described his own death and his after-life existence in some detail, as the following excerpt indicates.

> After breathing my last breath in my mortal body, I found myself in some sort of extension of existence that held no parallel, as far as I could estimate, in the material dimension I had recently experienced. . . . Now, here I was, still same I, with capacities to think and observe sharpened to an incredible degree. I felt earth-life suddenly very unreal almost as though it had never happened. It took me quite a long time to understand this feeling until I realized at

last that matter is certainly illusory although it does exist in actuality; the material world seemed now nothing more than a seething, changing restless sea of indeterminate density and volume. How could I have thought that that was reality, the last word of Creation to mankind? Yet it is understandable that the state in which a man exists, however temporary, constitutes the passing reality which is no longer reality when it has passed.[2]

A VIEW FROM THE SOURCE "SALUMET"

The second view from an extraordinary source is excerpted from the transcript of a series of sessions with trance mediums in Kingsclere, England. The principal entity channeled in these sessions was not a deceased human but an extraterrestrial intelligence who introduced himself as Salumet. Conversations with him, as well as with Bonniol, another extraterrestrial, were channeled by Eileen Roper, a full-trance medium, and Paul Moss, a partial-trance medium. Sarah Duncalf, a partial-trance medium, has also channeled other extraterrestrial entities. George Moss, the scientist who convened the sessions, was the lead questioner.* The principal points made in these voluminous conversations focus on the nature of consciousness, energy, and thought, and the possibility of communication across space and time.

MIND, SPIRIT, CONSCIOUSNESS

- Spirit has always been.
- All things are created first in the world of spirit, and then their counterparts are brought into physical existence.
- Mind/spirit/consciousness are fundamentally different from brain and all things in the physical world. Mind/spirit/consciousness are part of

---

*The complete transcript of the sessions has been published by George Moss in *The Chronicles of Aerah–Mind-link Communications Across the Universe,* 2009, and *Earth's Cosmic Ascendancy,* 2014.

the world of spirit, and as such they are instantly linked throughout space and time. The world of spirit extends throughout the space and time of this universe, and of all other universes. It has no space; in it all things are instantly linked.

ENERGY

- There is an "energetic void" extending throughout the universe. (But the term "void" is slightly misleading because it implies emptiness.) The energetic void has always been; it precedes the known universe: "it is part of creation." Spirit is associated with the energetic and changeable void: one cannot separate the two. Mind belongs to the world of spirit.

- While it is eternal, energy has the ability to change. It is never static. It is preferable to call it "aether." It is basically spiritual energy.

- Space, even in the absence of material atoms, is part of creation. All is energy, regardless of whether it is given a name or not.

- There are many different densities of energy (or of "energy waves"); some are yet to be discovered by human scientists.

THOUGHT

- Thought is the most powerful thing one can possess. It belongs to spirit. It has no weight; it is pure energy—it belongs to the energy of the whole of creation. That is why thought can travel throughout many universes in an instant—even more quickly than an instant! (But this is just to use physical concepts to explain it.) All is energy, but thought is a very different process. It is more refined.

COMMUNICATION (MIND-LINKS)

- Within spacetime nothing travels faster than the speed of light. But spirit is a domain that has no space, so that minds, wherever located in the physical universe, can simply link. Mind ignores physical distance.

- Spirit (mind, consciousness) is external to spacetime, so that mind-link communications are in no way compromised by physical distance—they are instantaneous (as in telepathy, prayer, and so on). Brain is physical and belongs to the spacetime world.
- Mind-links can operate at any physical distance, even beyond the observable universe. Physical distance is simply irrelevant to mind communications.
- An evolved mind can communicate with people before they are born and with relatives after they have died.
- There is no language problem in mind-link communication, because the receiver's brain can download the thought behind the words in its own language.

NOTES

CHAPTER 1.
NEAR-DEATH EXPERIENCES

1. Paul Storey, trans., *Plato: The Collected Dialogues,* Edith Hamilton and Huntington Cairns, eds. (Princeton University Press, 1989), "Republic X."
2. Michael B. Sabom, *Light and Death: One Doctor's Fascinating Account of Near-Death Experiences* (Grand Rapids, Mich.: Zondervan Publishing House, 1998).
3. Pim van Lommell, "About the Continuity of Our Consciousness," *Advances in Experimental Medicine and Biology* 550 (2004): 115–32.
4. Bruce Greyson, "Incidence and Correlates of Near-death Experiences in a Cardiac Care Unit," *General Hospital Psychiatry* 25, no. 4B (2003): 269–76.
5. Sam Parnia and Peter Fenwick, "Near-death Experiences in Cardiac Arrest: Visions of a Dying Brain or Visions of a New Science of Consciousness," *Resuscitation* 52 (2002): 5–11.
6. Jimo Borjigin, UnCheol Lee, Tiecheng Lui, et al., "Surge of Neurophysiological Coherence and Connectivity in the Dying Brain," *Proceedings of the National Academy of Science of the United States of America* (PNAS) 110, no. 35 (August 2013): 14432–37.
7. Henry Atherton, *The Resurrection Proved* (T. Dawes, 1680).
8. Ibid.
9. Albert Heim, "Notizen über den Tod durch Absturz," *Omega Magazine* 3 (1972): 45–52.
10. Ibid.

11. Kimberly Clark, "Clinical Interventions with Near-Death Experiencers," in *The Near-Death Experience: Problems, Prospects, Perspectives,* Bruce Greyson and Charles P. Flynn, eds. (Springfield, Ill.: Charles C. Thomas Publisher, 1984): 242–55.

12. Michael B. Sabom, *Light and Death: One Doctor's Fascinating Account of Near-Death Experiences* (Grand Rapids, Mich.: Zondervan Publishing House, 1998).

13. Ibid.

14. William L. Murtha, *Dying for Change; Survival, Hope and the Miracle of Choice* (Bloomington, Ind: Transformation Media Books, 2009).

15. Penny Sartori, Paul Badham, and Peter Fenwick, "A Prospectively Studied Near-Death Experience with Corroborated Out-of-Body Perceptions and Unexplained Healing," *Journal of Near-Death Studies* 25, no. 2 (2006): 69–84.

16. Ibid., 72.

17. Ibid., 73.

18. Ibid.

19. Ibid.

20. Amanda Cable, "Why The Day I Died Taught Me How To Live," *Daily Mail,* November 16, 2012.

21. Ibid.

CHAPTER 2. APPARITIONS AND AFTER-DEATH COMMUNICATION

1. Karlis Osis, *Deathbed Observations by Physicians and Nurses* (New York: The New York Parapsychology Foundation, 1961).

2. Edward F. Kelly, Adam Crabtree, Emily Williams Kelly, and Alan Gauld, *Irreducible Mind: Toward a Psychology for the 21st Century* (New York: Rowman & Littlefield Publishers Ltd., 2010), 409.

3. Allan L. Botkin, *Induced After-Death Communications* (Newburyport, Mass.: Hampton Roads Publishing Company, 2005).

4. Barbara Weisberg, *Talking to the Dead: Kate and Maggie Fox and the Rise of Spiritualism* (San Francisco: HarperSanFrancisco, 2004): 12–13.

5. Ibid.

6. Renée Haynes, *The Society for Psychical Research, 1882–1982: A History* (London: MacDonald & Co., 1982).

7. Eleanor Sidgwick and Alice Johnson, *Proceedings of the Society for Psychical Research* (SPR) Volume X (1894).

8. Edward Gurney and Frederick W. H. Myers, "On Apparitions Occurring Soon After Death," *Proceedings of the SPR* 5, Part XIV (1889): 403–86.

9. Ibid.

10. William F. Barrett, *Psychical Research* (Pomeroy, Wa.: Health Research Books, 1996): 124–27.

11. Ibid., 126.

12. Bruce Greyson, "Seeing Dead People Not Known to Have Died: 'Peak in Darien' Experiences," *Anthropology and Humanism* 35, no. 2 (2010): 165–66.

13. Robert Crookall, *Intimations of Immortality: Seeing That Led to Believing* (Cambridge: Lutterworth Press, 1965), 57.

14. Ibid.

15. Frances Power Cobbe, "Little's Living Age (5th series)," in *The Peak in Darien: The Riddle of Death* (1877), 374–79.

16. William F. Barrett, *Death-Bed Visions* (London: Methuen, 1926).

17. Donna Marie Sinclair, personal communication to Anthony Peake.

CHAPTER 3.
MEDIUM-TRANSMITTED COMMUNICATION

1. David Fontana, *Is There an Afterlife?* (London: O Books, 2005), 264.

2. Ibid., 150.

3. Richard Hodgson, "A Further Record of Observations of Certain Phenomena of Trance," *Proceedings of the Society for Psychical Research* (1897–8): 284–582.

4. Montague Keen, *Cross-Correspondences: An Introductory Note* (London: The Montague Keen Foundation, 2002).

5. Emily Williams Kelly, "Some Directions for Mediumship Research," *Journal of Scientific Exploration* 24, no. 2 (2010): 253.

6. E. J. Garrett, *Many Voices: The Autobiography of a Medium* (New York: Putnam, 1968).

7. Ibid.

8. Fontana, *Is There an Afterlife?*

9. Oliver Lodge, *Raymond or Life and Death* (New York: George H. Doran Company, 1916).

10. Fontana, *Is There an Afterlife?*, 194–95.

11. Ibid., 429.

12. K. Gay, "The Case of Edgar Vandy," *Journal of the Society for Psychical Research* 39, (1957): 49.

13. Fontana, *Is There an Afterlife?*, 194–95.

14. Guy Lyon Playfair and Montague Keen, "A Possibly Unique Case of Psychic Detection," *Journal of the Society for Psychical Research* 68, no. 1 (2004): 1–17.

15. Erlendur Haraldsson, "A Perfect Case? Emil Jensen in the Mediumship of Indriði Indriðason," *Proceedings of the Society for Psychical Research* 59, no. 223 (October 2011): 216.

16. Ibid.

17. Ibid.

18. Wolfgang Eisenbeiss and Dieter Hassler, "An assessment of Ostensible Communications with a Deceased Grand Master as Evidence for Survival," *Journal of the Society for Psychical Research* 70.2, no. 883 (April 2006): 65–97.

19. Ibid.

20. W. Stainton Moses, *Spirit Teachings* (Whitefish, Montana: Kessinger Publishing, 2004).

21. F. W. H. Myers, *Proceedings of the SPR* 9.25 (1894).

CHAPTER 4.
INSTRUMENTAL TRANSCOMMUNICATION

1. Waldemar Borogas, "The Chukchee," in Franz Boas, ed. *The Jesup North Pacific Expedition*, vol. 7, part II (New York: American Museum of Natural History, 1898–1903), 435.

2. George Noory and Rosemary Guiley, *Talking to the Dead* (New York: Tor Books, 2011).

3. Oscar d'Argonnel, *Vozes do Além pelo Telefone* (Rio de Janeiro: Pap. Typ. Marques, Araujo & C., 1925).

4. Anabela Cardoso, *Electronic Voices: Contact with Another Dimension?* (London: O Books, John Hunt Publishing Ltd., 2010): 29–30.

5. Friedrich Jürgenson, *The Voices from Space* (Stockholm: Saxon & Lindstrom, 1964).

6. Hans Bender, "Zur Analyse aussergewohnlicher Stimmphanomene auf Tonband. Erkundungsexperimente uber dir << Einspielungen >> von

Friedrich Jurgenson," *ZSPP (Zeitschrift für Parapsychologie und Grenzgebiete der Psychologie)* 12 (1970): 226–38.

7. Konstantin Raudive, *Breakthrough* (Gerrards Cross, U.K.: Colin Smythe Ltd., 1971).

8. Peter Bander, *Carry on Talking* (Gerrards Cross, U.K.: Colin Smythe Ltd., 1972).

9. David Fontana, *Is There an Afterlife?* (London: O Books, 2005), 361.

10. J. G. Fuller, *The Ghost of 29 Megacycles*. (London: Souvenir Press Ltd., 1985).

11. Anabela Cardoso, David Fontana, and Ernst Senkowski, "Experiment Transcript Only for Visiting Hans Otto König," *ITC Journal* 24 (2005).

12. Fontana, *Is There an Afterlife?*, 369.

13. Cardoso, *Electronic Voices,* 29–30.

14. Hans Bender, "On the Analysis of Exceptional Voice Phenomena on Tapes. Pilot Studies on the 'Recordings' of Friedrich Jürgenson," *ITC Journal* 40 (2011): 61–78.

15. Anabela Cardoso, "A Two-Year Investigation of the Allegedly Anomalous Electronic Voices or EVP," *Neuroquantology* 10, no. 3 (September 2012): 492–514.

16. Hildegard Schaefer, "Bridge between the Terrestrial and the Beyond: Theory and Practice of Transcommunication," www.worlditc.org/c_04_s_bridge_27.htm (accessed June 24, 2014).

17. Cardoso, *Electronic Voices,* 29–30.

18. Ervin Laszlo, *Quantum Shift in the Global Brain* (Rochester, Vt.: Inner Traditions, 2008), 153–56.

CHAPTER 5. PAST-LIFE RECOLLECTION

1. Carl-Magnus Stolt, "Hypnosis in Sweden during the Twentieth Century— The Life and Work of John Bjorkhem," *The History of Psychiatry* 15, no. 2 (June 2004): 193–200.

2. Albert de Rochas, *Les vies successives. Documents pour l'étude de cette question* (Paris: Bibliothèque Chacornac, 1911).

3. Ibid.

4. Morey Bernstein, *The Search for Bridey Murphy* (New York: Lancer Books, 1965), 303.

5. David Fontana, *Is There an Afterlife?* (London: O Books, 2004), 429.

6. Bernstein, *The Search for Bridey Murphy,* 303.

7. Roger Woolger, *Other Lives, Other Selves* (New York: HarperCollins, 1989).

8. Roger Woolger, "Beyond Death: Transition and the Afterlife," transcript of talk given at the Royal College of Psychiatrists, 2004.

9. Woolger, *Other Lives, Other Selves.*

CHAPTER 6. REINCARNATION

1. Alexander Cannon, *The Power Within* (London: Rider & Co., 1960).

2. Ian Stevenson, "The Evidence for Survival from Claimed Memories of Former Incarnations," *Journal of the American Society for Psychical Research* 54 (1958): 51–71.

3. Ian Stevenson, *Twenty Cases Suggestive of Reincarnation* (Charlottesville, Va.: University of Virginia Press, 1988).

4. Ian Stevenson, "The South-East Asian Interpretation of Gender Dysphoria: An Illustrative Case Report," *The Journal of Nervous and Mental Disease* 165, no. 3 (1977): 203.

5. Ibid.

6. Stevenson, *Twenty Cases Suggestive of Reincarnation.*

7. Ibid.

8. Ian Stevenson, *Children Who Remember Previous Lives: A Question of Reincarnation* (Charlottesville, Va.: University of Virginia Press, 1987).

9. Jim B. Tucker, "Children's Reports of Past-Life Memories," *Explore* 4, no. 4 (July/August 2008): 10.

10. Jim B. Tucker, *Life Before Life. A Scientific Investigation of Children's Memories of Previous Lives* (New York: St. Martin's Press, 2005).

11. Tucker, "Children's Reports of Past-Life Memories," 247.

12. Ian Stevenson and Satwant Pasricha, "A Preliminary Report on an Unusual Case of the Reincarnation Type with Xenoglossy," *Journal of the American Society for Psychical Research* 74 (1980): 331–48.

CHAPTER 7.
THE REDISCOVERY OF THE DEEP DIMENSION

1. Zeeya Merali, "The Universe Is a String-net Liquid," http://dao.mit.edu/~wen/NSart-wen.htm (accessed June 24, 2014).

2. Natalie Wolchover, "A Jewel at the Heart of Quantum Physics," www
.simonsfoundation.org/quanta/20130917-a-jewel-at-the-heart-of-quantum
-physics (accessed June 24, 2014).

3. Nima Arkani-Hamed, Jacob L. Bourjaily, Freddy Cachazo, et al., "Scattering
Amplitudes and the Positive Grassmannian," Cornell University Library,
2012, http://arxiv.org/abs/1212.5605 (accessed June 24, 2014); Nima Arkani-
Hamed and Jaroslav Trnka, "The Amplituhedron," Cornell University
Library, 2013, http://arxiv.org/abs/1312.2007 (accessed June 24, 2014).

4. E. Megidish, A. Halevy, T. Sachem, et al., "Entanglement Between
Photons That Have Never Coexisted," Physical Review Letters 110
(2013): 210403.

5. Masanori Hanada, Yoshifumi Hyakutake, Goro Ishiki, and Jun Nishimura,
"Holographic Description of Quantum Black Hole on a Computer," http://
arxiv.org/abs/1311.5607 (accessed June 24, 2014).

CHAPTER 8.
CONSCIOUSNESS IN THE COSMOS

1. Roger Penrose and Stuart Hameroff, "Orchestrated Reduction of Quantum
Coherence in Brain Microtubules: A Model for Consciousness," *Neural
Network World* 5, no. 5 (1995): 793–804.

2. Roger Penrose and Stuart Hameroff, "Orchestrated Reduction of Quantum
Coherence in Brain Microtubules: A Model for Consciousness," in *Toward
a Science of Consciousness—The First Tucson Discussions and Debates,* S.
R. Hameroff, A. Kaszniak and A. C. Scott, eds. (Cambridge, Mass.: MIT
Press, 1996).

CHAPTER 10. DEATH AND BEYOND:
THE RETURN TO THE AKASHA

1. Jane Sherwood, *The Country Beyond* (London: Rider & Co., 1945).

2. Sogyal Rinpoche, *The Tibetan Book of Living and Dying* (New York:
HarperCollins Publishers, 1993).

3. Virgil, *Aeneid* (Oxford, UK: Oxford University Press, 1940), 6:705 ff.

4. Poonam Sharma and Jim B. Tucker, "Cases of the Reincarnation Type with
Memories from the Intermission Between Lives," *Journal of Near Death
Studies* 23, no. 2 (Winter, 2004): 101–18.

5. Tulku Thondup, *Peaceful Death, Joyful Rebirth: A Tibetan Buddhist Guidebook* (Shambhala: Boston and London, 2006).

6. Jane Roberts, *Seth Reader* (San Anselmo, Calif.: Vernal Equinox Press, 1993).

APPENDIX. CONSCIOUS IMMORTALITY:
THE DAWN OF A NEW ERA

1. Rosemary Brown, *Immortals by My Side* (London: Bachman & Turner, 1974).

2. Ibid.

INDEX

BOOKS OF RELATED INTEREST

Science and the Akashic Field
An Integral Theory of Everything
by Ervin Laszlo

The Self-Actualizing Cosmos
The Akasha Revolution in Science and Human Consciousness
by Ervin Laszlo

The Akashic Experience
Science and the Cosmic Memory Field
by Ervin Laszlo

Dawn of the Akashic Age
New Consciousness, Quantum Resonance, and the Future of the World
by Ervin Laszlo and Kingsley L. Dennis

Morphic Resonance
The Nature of Formative Causation
by Rupert Sheldrake

Where Does Mind End?
A Radical History of Consciousness and the Awakened Self
by Marc Seifer, Ph.D.

Stalking the Wild Pendulum
On the Mechanics of Consciousness
by Itzhak Bentov

Science and the Afterlife Experience
Evidence for the Immortality of Consciousness
by Chris Carter

INNER TRADITIONS • BEAR & COMPANY
P.O. Box 388
Rochester, VT 05767
1-800-246-8648
www.InnerTraditions.com

Or contact your local bookseller